My Favourite Person

One In A Million
Edited by Aimée Vanstone

First published in Great Britain in 2009 by:

Young Writers
Young Writers
Remus House
Coltsfoot Drive
Peterborough
PE2 9JX
Telephone: 01733 890066
Website: www.youngwriters.co.uk

All Rights Reserved
Book Design by Spencer Hart & Tim Christian
© Copyright Contributors 2009
SB ISBN 978-1-84924-696-5

Foreword

Our 'My Favourite Person 2009' poetry competition attracted young aspiring poets to show their admiration for those who have made an impact in their life. What better way to let those closest know how much they are appreciated.

We are delighted to present 'One In A Million'. After reading through the hundreds of entries it is clear the amount of enthusiasm and love that went into writing these poems, therefore we hope you'll agree they are an inspiring and heart-warming read.

Young Writers was established in 1991 to promote poetry and creative writing to schoolchildren and encourage them to read, write and enjoy it. Here at Young Writers we are sure you'll agree that this special edition achieves our aim and celebrates today's wealth of young writing talent. We hope you enjoy 'One In A Million' for many years to come.

Contents

Bryony Porter-Collard (15)	1
Laura Jane Flaherty (11)	2
Shelee Carbon (5)	2
Cassie Ramos-Stovin (11)	3
Anna Harrison (9)	3
Machaela Tapper (10)	4
Rhys Williams (5)	4
Rebecca Strangward (12)	5
India Collins (11)	6
Juny Maria Jose (12)	7
Shannon Alice Burton (11)	8
Daniel Mitchell (11)	9
Rebecca Meredith (6)	9
Jade Pickett (14)	10
Iwan McCullough (10)	10
Alice Chambers (10)	11
Brooke Clarke (10)	11
Sia Umu Ndomaina (11)	12
Megan Jones (9)	12
Natasha Wilkinson (9)	13
Sasha Dixon (10)	13
Gadi Schleider (10)	14
Amina Khatun (11)	14
Violentin Vukelaj (11)	15
Levi Holt (14)	15
Chloe Adshead (10)	16
Josh Leatham (11)	16
Jennifer Olsen (11)	17
Lauren Peachment (10)	17
Nyrah Saleem (12)	18
Chloe Hamilton (7)	18
Alicia Chloe Gee (11)	19
Nathan Sweeney (11)	19
Alice Wilson (10)	20
Natalie Sterland (11)	20
Fozia Patel (11)	21
Dominic Robertson (10)	21
Colleen Gorman (10)	22
Lauren McHardy (11)	22
Jessica Wright (11)	23
Scarlet Nolan (6)	23
Rebecca Little (11)	24
Sarah Bowles (11)	24
Emily Cross (9)	25
Jake Crump (11)	25
John Bates (9)	26
Sunaina Rana (10)	26
Hayley Stronge (11)	27
Brianna Connolly (11)	27
Monwara Bibi (11)	28
Zyra Yaseen (11)	28
Charlea-Anne Thompson (11)	29
Hannah Horvath (10)	29
Lauren Read (10)	30
Khayroon Suleyman (10)	30
Mandeep Hayer (11)	31
Flora Maycock (10)	31
Ashlin Watts (10)	32
Tamara Elms (11)	32
Imogen Walsh (10)	33
Zoe Straw (10)	33
Sophie Francis (10)	34
Chloe Tamara Johnson (11)	34
Veronica Faluyi (11)	35
Jack Greaves (9)	35
Amy Parker (10)	36
Declan Ingledew (11)	36
Sarah Titterington (12)	37
Katie McComiskey (6)	37
Ella Seaborn (10)	38
Zara Kauser (11)	38
Nicola Jeffs (11)	39
Jasmine Lauren Hope (8)	39
Millie Cresdee (10)	40
Eloise Hillier (10)	40
Eleanor Gladman (11)	41
Chardonae Stephenson (11)	41
Suzie Frith (11)	42
Katherine Stanley (9)	42
Abbie Weatherill (10)	43
Charlie Taylor (9)	43
Meadhbh Murphy (11)	44

Holly Bate (6)	44
Hannah Sawitzki (11)	45
Visha Arfan (12)	45
Sacha Davies (11)	46
Faye McDonald (8)	46
Caleb Kennelly (11)	47
Mai Tumber (9)	47
La'Raib Kamran Wayn (11)	48
Sam Jones (12)	48
Matthew Robinson (10)	49
Charlotte Williams (11)	49
Sian Matthew (11)	50
Alisha Pandya (10)	50
William Fedorov (10)	51
Nathan Crane (11)	51
Mathangi Sritharan (9)	52
Eleasha Tahnee Makin (11)	52
Charlotte Balls (11)	53
Kelsey Clifford (10)	53
Rebecca Scaife (10)	54
Amy Chandler (10)	54
Ellah Jackson (10)	55
Emily Dalton (10)	55
Maddy Matthews (15)	56
Kainat Abed (11)	56
Amy Jones (10)	57
Kieran Morton (11)	57
Ahmed Mohammed (10)	58
Sophie Hannah Rowberry (11)	58
Felicia Martino (8)	59
Zoe Holloway (10)	59
Hollie Hopkisson (9)	60
Thomas Atherton (11)	60
Lucy Stanhope (11)	61
Olivia Jarvis (11)	61
Ruby Crowhurst (11)	62
Charlotte Preece (12)	62
Holly Marie Port (11)	63
Rebecca Ann Rigby (10)	63
Ruhi Ur-Rashid (14)	64
Katy Strong (11)	64
Abbie Storer (8)	65
Amy Smith (9)	65
Hannah Chow (11)	66
Dawn Claire Parsons (10)	66
Caitlin Burton (11)	67
Maniba Kiani (11)	67
Zoe Wilson (11)	68
Emily Lambourne (9)	68
Alexandra Drysdale (11)	69
Adam Allaway (9)	69
Kirsty Wishart (11)	70
Clayton Ryan (11)	70
Shona Macdonald (11)	71
Sajida Desai (10)	71
Jordan Moores (12)	72
Zara Khan (9)	72
Molly Faulkner (12)	73
Rebekah Whitnell (11)	73
Eoin Coulter (10)	74
Emma Wagstaff (10)	74
Mathilda Bassnett (10)	75
Annie Smith (9)	75
Mollie Nixon (8)	76
Bianca Walker (15)	76
Brandon Dudley (11)	77
Faheema Shaikh (11)	77
Lillian-Mae Nuttall (10)	78
Maria Chesnaye (10)	78
Bailey Corbett (9)	79
Anna McCoy (9)	79
James Allbrook (10)	80
Amreena Kaur (11)	80
Lily Temple (11)	81
Farhana Begum (10)	82
Erin Scorgie (11)	82
Lindsey McIlwaine (10)	83
Leanna Bradbury (11)	83
Sian Farai Chinamora (8)	84
Kraig Wymer-Webb (11)	84
Ellie Bulloch (10)	85
Bryan Letters (11)	85
Nadine Foster (11)	86
Annie Goulding (8)	86
Alex Anna Mackay (7)	87
Heather Addison (11)	87
Joshua Andrew Foakes (10)	88
Katrina Newlyn (10)	88
Tyler Parry (7)	89
Alicia Chapman (10)	89

Kassi Watson (11)	90
Cameron MacReady (9)	90
Olivia Blanks (10)	91
Niamh Walls (8)	91
Grace Hopkinson (11)	92
Aaron Vittles (11)	92
Liza Koroleva (11)	93
Jamie Cooke (10)	93
Francesca Slattery (12)	94
Holly Douch (10)	94
Lucy MacDonald (11)	95
Malik Shahzad Khan (8)	95
Katrina May (9)	96
Megan Hughes (11)	96
Caitlyn Michelle Kirby (10)	97
Benjamin Hartshorne (11)	97
Ella Turney (11)	98
Ryan Brown (10)	98
Mark Bell (9)	99
Rhys Langley (9)	99
Rebecka Barwood (11)	100
Rhiannon Morgan (8)	100
Lauren Drysdale (11)	101
Hannah Clarke (8)	101
Jack Riley (10)	102
Aaron Karn (11)	102
Ryan Leatherland (9)	103
Sydney Clay (9)	103
Kristian Lacey (11)	104
Georgia Hunt (11)	104
Callum Donelan (11)	105
Rosa McManners (10)	105
Chloe Godding (11)	105
Anukiraha Uthayarajan (10)	106
George Stefan Acquaah (10)	106
Demi Allan (10)	106
Holly Neary-King (10)	107
Katie Button-Williams (11)	107
Lilly Grant (10)	107
Kathy McTeague (12)	108
Maisie Dyson (11)	108
Joe McGarry (9)	108
Courtney Aston (10)	109
Kirsten Perie (11)	109
Alexandra McMullen (11)	110
Carl Knight (10)	110
Lucy Lewin (7)	111
Olivia Leah Donaghue (9)	111
Sophie Domingo (9)	112
Megan Vest (10)	112
Eve Allan (9)	113
Stacey Graham (11)	113
Katie Michelle Marder (11)	113
Lucy Hickman (9)	114
Daniel Robinson (11)	114
Ashleigh Roberts (10)	114
Ellis Scott (8)	115
Tanya Brown (9)	115
Charlotte Travers (7)	115
Crystal Tueneboah (10)	116
Annalise Cabrera (12)	116
Amy Pritchard (10)	116
Harriet Barlow (11)	117
Matthew Smyth (9)	117
Jessica Hatton (11)	117
Liam Robinson (11)	118
Matilda Hancock (10)	118
Charlotte Perry (10)	118
Emily Williams (10)	119
Courtney Hughes (9)	119
Chloe Ball (11)	119
Emily Forbes (11)	120
Jerry Durocher-Morris (10)	120
Mirriam Morson (10)	120
Sukhraj Puwar (12)	121
Elizabeth Brunt (10)	121
Leah Girvan (9)	121
Darren Slater (8)	122
Liam Sharland (11)	122
Jessica Badham (10)	122
Jonathan David Morris (9)	123
Kasie Szilak (10)	123
Kyle Stratford (11)	123
Natasha Newton (10)	124
Katie Sperring (6)	124
Emily Grace Seeds (10)	124
Kayleigh Gibson (10)	125
Nicola Finch (10)	125
Sam Young (10)	125
Sam Callway (11)	126

- Francesca Johnson (10)..........................126
- Shannon Jewell (10)...............................126
- Holly Gregory (10) 127
- Gena-Leigh McNeice (11) 127
- Niamh Berridge-Burley (9)....................127
- Freya Lewin (6) 128
- Cailet Latham (11) 128
- Alexia Dawson (6) 128
- Lucy Christian (10).................................129
- Emily Wallace (11) 129
- Rebekah Griffiths (9)............................129
- Chloe Hawcroft (10).............................130

The Poems

Just Like A Twin

My favourite person is always there for me
Always laughing she makes me feel so free
She lifts me up when I am down
Never want to say goodbye
Never want to see her frown

I am only really me when I'm with her
I feel so happy, that's for sure
Crazy we may be, well we are
But I swear when I'm with her
I can touch the stars

She's a one in a million friend
Going to be always laughing
We'll be friends till the end

And when I do take my final breath
She's all I'll see
All the memories still fresh
In my mind where they'll forever be

I got to make every moment count
'Cause you never know what could happen
But there's no doubt
She's the best friend I'll ever meet
All these times I'll forever keep

Never going to leave when she needs me
I'll always come for her
But only if she asks me

We make the best team
Always going to win
This feeling is so strong
She's more than a friend,
She's my twin!

Bryony Porter-Collard (15)

My Nan Rules

My nice, noble nanny,
We're not allowed to call her Granny,
She says, 'That name is for someone old.'
But not my nan, she's young, she's bold.
You should see her dance,
It's such a picture,
Unfortunately, her and rhythm are not a tasty mixture.
We gave her two baby guinea pigs,
She viewed them as precious as the finest pearls,
But little did she know, they were not boys, they were girls.
She named them Wheatan and Brandon,
The names of the place where she lives.
But what we love the most about her,
Is the warm love she gives.
My nan grew up and had eight children, including my mum,
So she keeps a secret weapon
For when cheekiness comes from anyone.
Now I'm being truthful here,
She couldn't hurt a fly,
When she tries to smack us,
We laugh, not cry.
The funny thing is that she laughs too,
We could probably get away with murder,
Unless we take 1 out of 200 of her cool high-heeled shoes.
My nan loves to shop,
She could literally shop until she drops,
Her room is full of make-up, clothes, teddies and jewels.
Yeah, my nan's so awesome, she rocks, man, she rules!

Laura Jane Flaherty (11)

My Favourite Person

My favourite person is Sian.
She plays with me and shares her toys.
She is my best friend.

Shelee Carbon (5)

The King Of Pop – Acrostic

M ichael Jackson is still No 1
I t's true there will be no one so great,
C hildren and adults still worship his music,
H aving had such a horrible fate.
A nyone felt honoured to be in his presence,
E ven little children so small,
L ikeable with great music and so very kind,

J ackson had it all!
A nd then the press started to write
C ruel and untrue tales,
K ind was he, yet the stories so bad,
S till the press tried to make sure he failed,
O ne by one the fans go on,
N ever will the number of supporters drop,
S o still to this very day he's called:

T he King of Pop!
R umours prove nothing, they're just stories,
I t's the music the people want to hear,
B ut the rumours hurt his very heart,
U ntil his mission was so very clear.
T he songs he performed each had a message,
E very message was so strong,

P eople would try and put his messages into action,
O n top of everything that went wrong.
E veryone has a special idol,
M ine is Michael Jackson.

Cassie Ramos-Stovin (11)

Anna Wright

We do some dancing, up high and down low.
We sing some songs about the fun we have.
Now we go swimming and play games for free.
That's the way for Anna and me.

Anna Harrison (9)

My Favourite Person

I am sitting here thinking.
On this rainy day.
Of my favourite person.
It's hard to pick.
It's hard to say.
Who is my favourite person from day to day.

One day it's my mum.
Hip hip hooray.
She is in the running.
Only on a good day.

Next I've got my nan.
Who loves me.
Is she my favourite?
We will have to wait and see.

Then there's my dad.
He's special to me.
Don't know whether he's my favourite
But he could be.

My grandad is next, well what can I say?
My grandad's my grandad
In a special way.

Then there's someone I haven't mentioned at all.
He is my brother Wyatt
He's not very tall.
But I think he is my favourite one of all.

Machaela Tapper (10)

My Favourite Person

My favourite person is my mummy
Because she looks after me.
She gives me sweets
When I am good at the weekend.

Rhys Williams (5)

My Fluffy, Little Friend

There!
A jet-black puffball was lying on Mum's bed,
It opened its eyes and scratched its head.
White tips like cotton socks on its paws and belly.
I reached out to stroke it, my arm felt like jelly.
It was soft to the touch with velvety fur,
With a deep, rippling, loveable purr.
I lay awake with wonderful ideas in my head,
Like collars and toys and name tags and beds.
I woke up at midnight to see her one more time,
Tiptoeing carefully, I saw eyes of lime.
When I got there I picked it up, as light as a feather,
As beautiful as a heather.
I took it into my room and it lay on my duvet,
I told it all my secrets and about my day.
I said things like:
'When you arrived it was too good to be true!
I can't even imagine being a cat like you!'
We play together,
We lay together.
It may not be human but it's still my favourite pet,
We rescued it from being abandoned and that I'll never forget.
I trust it so much,
I love it so much
And it loves me.
Its name is Kitty.
My fluffy, little friend.

Rebecca Strangward (12)

More Than Money Can Buy

This is a story about a girl,
A girl as pretty as a pearl.
So I will start,
With words from the heart.
She's more than money can buy!

So it's official,
She's super special
As you may see.
She means the world to me,
She's more than money can buy!

I knew her when
We were babies back then.
Sitting in the grass,
We did nothing but laugh.
She's more than money can buy!

Then when we were three,
It was oh, tragedy!
She moved away,
I thought of her every day.
She's more than money can buy!

I've seen her again,
We've long passed ten.
What will the future hold
When we are old?
Katie's more than money can buy!

India Collins (11)

Jude In Mood For Fun

My little kitty is Jude,
Always in a good mood,
She's a cute little dude,
Always in a funny mood,
She eats all her food.

She's white and small,
Always in the hall,
Funny when she rolls
On her little ball,
But she never falls.

She doesn't like dark,
She goes to the park,
To watch a lark,
Near Mr Clark
And a dog who barks.

One day she'll be a cat,
Never be scared of a rat,
She'll be sitting on a mat,
She won't be fat,
Wearing my nice hat.

She likes to play
On a sunny day,
She knows what I say,
We went to see a bay,
On a day in May.

Juny Maria Jose (12)

Mum

My mum is my favourite person,
She's so lovely, bubbly and bright,
And when I feel upset,
She's bound to put things right!
My mum is extremely kind,
Helping me get things off my mind,
She is also very caring,
And is always nicely sharing.
My mum buys me lollies,
When I'm feeling hot,
Then we make a fruit salad,
And put it in a pot.
My mum plays swing ball with me,
And takes me swimming too,
Then after getting dressed and dry
I say, 'Mum, there's nothing I'd rather do,
Than be with you!'

So my mum is my favourite person,
For all of these reasons,
And a million and one more
But to write all these
Would take all the seasons!
My mum is my favourite,
And I love her so
And I want to be with her,
Wherever she might go!

Shannon Alice Burton (11)

My Mum

The person I have chosen
For this topic is my mum
Because she is so bright
So lovely and so fun!

She always cares for me
She always makes me happy
From the moment I was born
To me wearing a nappy!

When I come home from school
I receive kisses and hugs
A refreshing glass of cocoa
Each day in different mugs!

She makes my breakfast
Lunch and tea
She doesn't give me too much
She knows how to look after me!

She is my best friend
And will always be
I love her more and more each day
Just as she loves me!

Her bright blue eyes
And flowing locks
Lovely soft skin
My mum *rocks!*

Daniel Mitchell (11)

My Favourite Person

My favourite friend is Katie
She loves to bark a lot
She is black and white
She likes to chase cats
Can you guess what my favourite friend is . . . ?

Rebecca Meredith (6)

Idolisation

They swish their way across the pitch
And trick the opposing team,
They sing to the world in harmony
And are always to be seen.

They strut their stuff across the dance floor
Making tapping and bopping noises,
They talk aloud to the listening world
And make a lot of difficult choices.

We look up to lots of idols
Most of us not knowing,
That the true idols in our lives
Are the ones that brought us up.

They love you with all their heart
And will try to never let you down,
They will protect you from all that's bad
And will never want to see you frown.

They will fight your battles
And will always stand up for you,
They care so much
And want you to get the best in everything you do.

We look up to lots of idols
Most of us not knowing,
That the true idols in our lives
Are the ones that brought us up.

Jade Pickett (14)

My Mum

My mum is busy like a bee
As slow as a snail
and kind as can be
but still has time for me
and the rest of the family!

Iwan McCullough (10)

My Monster

My monster is fierce,
But he protects me
When I'm in deep tears.
He is beautiful,
Made of pure love,
He is dutiful.

My monster is brilliant,
As you can plainly see.
More or less,
He acts like you and me.

My monster is kind,
In every single way,
He has a special mind
That keeps me alive today.
He's my best friend,
Our relationship could never bend!

My monster is brilliant,
As you can plainly see.
More or less,
He acts like you and me.

My monster is fierce,
He has a great mind,
My monster is like me,
One of a kind.

Alice Chambers (10)

My Dog, Kie

He likes to eat most pies
He sometimes wears ties
And he has little brown eyes

And when I am not there he sometimes cries
Because he was my first surprise.

Brooke Clarke (10)

Mum

She scurries around the house,
Tidies up the rooms,
No speck of dirt could hide away,
No flake of dust could survive,
When she is nearby with her cleaning supplies,
She moves around rapidly,
When she is searching,
High and low for dirt and dust.

She has arms for me to snuggle into,
On a cold winter night,
And sings a joyful tune to lighten up my day,
Her smile comforts me,
As I drift towards the moon.

She knows when I'm up to mischief,
And knows when trouble is about,
She senses it all without me telling her,
As though she can read me like a book.

She is there when I need her,
Through thick and thin,
She's like the wind beneath my wings,
There to carry me when I fall,
I'm very lucky you know,
But not because she does all these things for me,
But because I have a wonderful mum like her!

Sia Umu Ndomaina (11)

Sweet Tayla Lily

Tayla Lily is so sweet
All the way down to her cute little feet.
She is my sister and is so small
And is loved so much by us all.
Although she screams and rolls about
We hardly ever have to shout.

Megan Jones (9)

My Mam – The Greatest

My mam is sweet
She gives me treats,
My mam is helpful
And treats me well,
She is kind
Bear that in mind,
When she's poorly
She is truly,
When she's well
You can tell,
She smells sweet
Unlike her feet,
She thinks it's cool
When I'm at school,
When she's at work
I smirk,
When I'm in the bath
She's having a laugh,
When my dad's drinking beer
She gives him a sneer,
She works hard for money,
So we can go places when it's sunny,
When I go out
My mam shouts,
She's my mam and she's the greatest!

Natasha Wilkinson (9)

My Favourite Person

My favourite person is someone who makes me laugh
My favourite person is someone who is there for me
My favourite person is someone who stops me worrying
My favourite person is someone I can have fun with
My favourite person is my
                Best friend!

Sasha Dixon (10)

My Cheeky Little Brother

My little brother, Myer,
He loves looking at fire,
He gobbles up all on his plate,
And has lots of little mates,
With a cheeky grin,
He looks through the bin,
He is like a broken tape recorder
Not knowing when to stop,
He also enjoys playing and tossing the mop,
He splashes in the bath,
Oh how he giggles and laughs,
He messes up my games,
And has a really cute name.
He hates it in his bed,
And is very well fed.
He wobbles when he walks,
And really tries to talk,
He loves it in the pool,
And I think he is very cool,
He is adorable when he sleeps,
And has lots of toys he keeps,
He likes to look up,
And always drinks from a cup,
He is loved by us in all his moods,
Two is his age so don't forget it dudes!

Gadi Schleider (10)

You Can Always Trust A Friend

A friend is who you trust and they trust you back.
They are always there for you and never let you down.
They are special because you don't get given them
You choose them.
They like you for who you are
And that's why you can trust your friend.

Amina Khatun (11)

The One In A Million

My favourite person is my best friend, Jerome,
Because whenever I'm feeling down in the dumps,
He makes things to cheer me up,
Whenever Jerome or I go home,
Or on the way to a football match,
There is never a dull moment with Jerome around,
Yes it might get on my nerves when he speaks about Germany,
And all about the food there too much,
But sometimes it can get interesting.
And who knows it might come in handy in the future,
He taught me some words in German
And I found it so interesting
That I went and bought a CD to learn German.
Jerome is kind, helpful, generous and cheerful,
This all reminds me of the time
Me and Jerome were coming back from a football match,
And we got lost on the way home,
But we were with our mums
So at the end we did find our way home,
But it was mad, running from one bus stop to the next,
Me and Jerome loved it.
It was the best day ever.
And all these things and all this is why I think,
Jerome is the one in a million.

Violentin Vukelaj (11)

My Mum

When shadows are nearing,
Or I fail to make a jump,
Or if I can't see light at the end of the tunnel,
I look behind me and see my mum,
I know she will give me reassurance, confidence,
She's the only person I know will never judge me,
I love my mum!

Levi Holt (14)

The Person I Adore

My favourite person is my grandad
But he isn't as you'd think.
He isn't old and wrinkly
And hates the colour pink.

His name is David Connor,
His age is fifty-two.
Though he acts like he is thirty-five,
You should see what he can do.

He supports Man United,
And loves football, in fact.
He is a referee, window cleaner and a player,
With his strength still intact.

Sometimes he takes me swimming,
Really anywhere.
Sometimes I think that he and I,
We make the perfect pair.

I don't care that he wears glasses,
I don't care that he's bald.
I love my grandad . . . so with him I . . .
Do as I'm told!

David really is the person I adore!

Chloe Adshead (10)

Ben Is The Best

He's my best friend,
His name is Ben,
We always hang out together
In our den,
He is very nice,
And would always give you good advice
I'll always be his friend,
And our friendship will never end.

Josh Leatham (11)

My Fave Peeps

I have so many,
It's very hard to choose,
I really couldn't pick one,
Because the others would all lose.
I have a very long list, of every nominee,
I wonder who my favourite is destined to be.
There's Dad, my protector,
There's Mr Nixon, my friend,
Then there's Mum, my teacher,
On her I can depend.
There's my nanna and grandad,
And Margaret too.
So many people,
What shall I do?
I've finally decided who it's going to be,
My very favourite person is definitely me!
As I'm the daughter of my parents,
A friend of my friends,
I hope you don't get muddled up
From the message that this sends.
I am a part of everyone,
Who's on my favourites list,
If I ever go away they will all be surely missed.

Jennifer Olsen (11)

My Favourite Person

My favourite person is in my family,
They are very good at looking after me,
They are very close to my heart,
And they play a very important part,
This person I can rely on,
I don't know what I'll do when they're gone,
This person is my mum,
Her cooking is yum.

Lauren Peachment (10)

My Mum – My Favourite Person

My mum is my favourite person,
There are many reasons why,
But here are some of them.

Every time she walks in the room,
My mind dozes off in a zoom.
Here and there she gets mad,
But when she looks at me she's never sad.

My mum is so kind,
So kind she can make me blind.
Whenever she is near,
No one comes with fear.

I love her so much,
She gives the greatest touch.
I also can't forget,
She makes the greatest food
That's why I'm always in a lovely mood.

Everyone likes her a lot
There's no reason for people to not.
I don't want to leave my mum
Never until the future comes.
This is why she's my favourite person!

Nyrah Saleem (12)

My Sister And I

M y sister is called Kylah Hamilton, she is one.
Y ou would love to see her.
S he is very small, cute and funny.
I love her very much.
S he makes me giggle, always getting into mischief.
T ogether we are best friends.
E very day we have lots of fun playing.
R un, run, here comes trouble!

Chloe Hamilton (7)

My Dad

I love my dad, he's special to me
Kind, loving and cuddly
When I was little
I would splash around in the bath
My dad would keep an eye on me
And I would make him laugh.

My dad's the best
And if I am good
I get treats from the shop
Nearly all the while.
Dad reminds me
The money tree in the garden is almost bare
As he gives me a smile.

I love the night-time
It's just the best
Me and Dad watching TV
All cuddled up on our settee.

My dad's funny when we go out in the car
He pulls faces at me in his mirror to make me laugh
I wouldn't swap my dad for a million and a half.

Me and my dad.

Alicia Chloe Gee (11)

Chris, My Brother

He's young and funny,
Never quiet, always loud,
He's my special brother,
And of that I'm proud.

At night when we go to bed,
And it's time to sleep,
He'll pop his head out of the covers,
And have a peep.

Nathan Sweeney (11)

Luckiest Girl

She is not only my best friend.
She is my mum too.
Always there for me,
If I am happy, she is happy too.
I know that she sometimes shouts at me.
But that is what mums do.
If I am sad, had a bad day at school,
Friends being mean to me.
I may come home upset and cry.
I know she is sad too,
She tries not to show it
She wipes away my tears,
Tells me it will be alright
And I know she will sort it out.
Because that is her job,
To love, care and look after me.
To teach me right from wrong.
She says if she could she would
Wrap me up in cotton wool.
We both know that is not possible.
I have got to grow up
And be responsible for my own life one day.

Alice Wilson (10)

Joe Jonas

Performing concerts on the stage,
With young girls screaming, cos he's on his way.

Writing songs with Demi and Miley,
I think it makes him very smiley.

His beautiful voice stuns everyone who listens,
No wonder he's sold lots of albums, but not quite millions.

Don't forget there are two others,
And together they are the Jonas Brothers.

Natalie Sterland (11)

Sisters 4-Ever!

My sister is sixteen,
She's phenomenal and unique,
She's older than me,
But we still make a good team.

We have our late-night talks
Which are private of course,
She makes me laugh by telling jokes
And backs me up in front of my folks.

We have our ups, we have our downs,
But mostly we're on straight grounds,
We have a strong relationship
That turns the frowns around.

My sister is my role model,
She's the one I look up to,
I'd love to be like her one day,
And if you meet her so might you!

Without my sister, where would I be?
I need her that's for sure,
Although sometimes I hate her guts,
She's my favourite person for evermore!

Fozia Patel (11)

My Feline Friend Hoffner

My feline friend Hoffner is a handsome tabby,
He can even handle my little cousin Callie,
He likes getting fed by our neighbour Ally,
My feline friend Hoffner is a handsome tabby.

Oh how I love my feline friend Hoffner,
He snuggles into my head,
He's my own living pillow,
I hope he lives as long as Grandmother Willow,
Oh how I love my feline friend Hoffner.

Dominic Robertson (10)

My Family

Cute and cuddly
White as snow
Paw prints everywhere
Little boy Charlie goes,

Elegant Emma
Dances around
Playing with her toys
That she has found,

The plumber of the house
Goes to fix everything,
Also he has to work all day
To pay the bills we've to pay,

Little miss chef
Cooks 3 meals a day
Keeping us living in every
Single way,

Finally it's me, what have I got to say
Well . . . I'm the drama queen
Everything's got to be perfect
As can be . . . for me!

Colleen Gorman (10)

I Love My Favourite Person

My favourite person:
Is a happy person,
Always out-going and smiling,
Party animal, happy, caring.

My favourite person:
Is always caring for me,
Is one of the best people in the world,
Lovely, nice, smart,
Her name is Amanda Noble.

Lauren McHardy (11)

How To Choose

Hmm, my favourite person,
Well, how to choose?
Who knows how many people,
By saying I could lose.

There's Mum, Dad,
Brother and sis.
With all of these people,
My life is just bliss.

There are nans, grandads,
Grans and grandpas.
Some of my favourite people,
Are even big stars.

There are cousins,
Aunties, uncles and pets,
The more lovely people,
The better it gets.

So you see my problem,
I love everyone.
But where I feel safest
Is with my dad and my mum.

Jessica Wright (11)

My Favourite Person

My favourite person is my mum
Together we have so much fun,
We go rock climbing at the beach,
She lifts me up when I can't reach,
Mum packs my lunch with yummy things,
My favourite being Cheesy Strings,
If I get hurt and start to cry,
Mum makes it better and that is why

     I love my mum

Scarlet Nolan (6)

The A, B, C

A mazing
N ice
N eat
A ngel

        B right
        R ascal
        O bedient
        N aughty
        A nimal lover

C aring
A ngelic
I ndependent
T alker
R ebel
I nquisitive
O bserving
N eighbour
A dorable

I had to write three for my three best friends
and let's hope these friendships never end.

Rebecca Little (11)

My Dad

My dad is old
And is always moaning about the weather being cold
He is funny and kind
When I ask him for his opinion anyone might think he is blind
He gives me kisses and cuddles
And fills my bath with nice-smelling bubbles
We have our chats about how much we love each other
He also has chats with my older brother
If I had to tell him how much he means to me
The answer would be wider than the oceans and all of the sea!

Sarah Bowles (11)

My Favourite Person

Grandad
Yes that's who.
He loves me loads,
And tells me loads.
That he's very lucky
To have me.

But I always say,
That it's the other way round,
That I'm the one
Who's so lucky.

He's there for me,
Through ups and downs,
There to guide me,
The right way round.

Let's not forget,
The presents too,
Money, toys, games.
I love you, Grandad
Very much indeed.
Thank you!

Emily Cross (9)

Dad!

My favourite person
Curry chomper,
Chilli eater,
Dog walker,
Sweet giver,
Long distance driver,
Bedroom painter,
Ebay seller,
Beer brewer,
That's my lovely, funny dad!

Jake Crump (11)

The Naughty Boys

Grandad is great,
and I am too,
we make up the 'Naughty Boys',
and this is what we do.

I like Grandad in the car,
he shouts at people near and far,
and when we're out for a trip
all we eat is sweets and chips.

At water balloons Grandad's ace,
he always gets Nanny in the face,
I wish I were as good as he,
he says, 'One day you'll be!'

Grandad's teaching me to play darts,
sing rude songs
and build go-karts.

He always lets me stay up late,
and tells my mum I was in bed by eight!

Maybe he's not the best influence on me
but when we're together I'm always happy!

John Bates (9)

My Sister

She makes me cry but then makes me laugh,
I call her silly, she calls me daft.
We would play games,
Then call each other names
We would often start a fight
Then hug by midnight,
I love her and I know she loves me
I think she is a star,
She shows she cares and makes things fun,
My sister will always be my number one.

Sunaina Rana (10)

My Favourite Person

My favourite person
Is my pet cockatiel, Coco,
He makes me laugh with chirps and tweets
And his feathers give a shiny glow.

I remember the day I bought him
We brought him home in a box, in the car,
And when we put him in his cage
I knew he was my special star.

He likes all my family
Especially Granda Jim,
But there's so much more about Coco
Here's a verse to describe him;

Perch sleeper, loud cheeper,
Mirror poser, never a closer,
Happy smiler, nail filer,
Noises and never a word, my bird,

He can't speak yet
But never say never,
He's my Coco forever and ever.

Hayley Stronge (11)

My Mum

My mum inspires me to do what I want,
She encourages me to stand up for myself when people taunt.
She's kind and gentle and always cares,
When I'm on the bus she pays my fares.
My mum comforts me when I am scared,
If she won (not gonna happen) the lottery
I know it would be shared.
My mum is great in so many ways,
She lights up the sun with her beautiful rays.

I love my mum!

Brianna Connolly (11)

My Favourite Person

My favourite person is imaginative,
We pretend we're hunters,
Searching for wild animals.

My favourite person is funny,
He tells great jokes,
He cheers me up when I'm upset.

My favourite person is playful,
We run around chasing each other,
So much fun we have together.

My favourite person is the *best!*
Always listening to what I say,
He always says the truth,
He never lies.

My favourite person is generous,
Always helping people.

    My favourite person is . . .
               My brother!
    Thank you for being such a great brother!

Monwara Bibi (11)

My Perfect Person

My mum makes me smile
She makes me worthwhile.

When I'm down
She turns my frown the right way round.

My mum is my perfect person
Because she'll always be there for me.

When I fall in a puddle
She gives me a cuddle.

My perfect person is my mum.

Zyra Yaseen (11)

My Uncle Simon

My Uncle Simon is my mum's brother
and the best uncle you could have,
he lets me ride in his sports car,
now I'm the coolest girl at school!
He plays with me on the Wii and
even bought one to practise on,
he'll be the fittest uncle around!
He went horse riding with me,
even though he was scared, *brave!*
He's taken me on a skiing holiday high up
in the mountains, now I was the brave one!
He let me take him ice skating,
he had never done it before, he was seriously
frightened of breaking something!
He buys me awesome things for my birthday
and Christmas - they really are cool!
And finally he takes me out for meals
when I see him.

I love him to bits and he would do anything
for me, he really is *my favourite person!*

Charlea-Anne Thompson (11)

My Favourite Things

My favourite thing is dancing,
My favourite snacks are crisps,
And my other favourite thing is having farmyard trips.

My favourite thing is basketball,
My favourite drink is tea,
My least most favourite thing is a busy buzzy bee.

My favourite thing is my pet dog,
My favourite show is 'Doctor Who',
And of all my favourite things in my life,
My favourite thing is you.

Hannah Horvath (10)

Mum's The Favourite

Mums are the world,
They mean a lot,
Whenever you're down,
They act like a clown,
But only to make you better.

Mums are for protection,
For love and full attention.
It's always what we like,
She's caring and sweet,
But not to eat,
Because I care and love her a lot.

My mum can cook,
But not just out of any old book,
It's fresh, it's nice,
But it's not what you would like,
Because she makes it especially for me.

So hands off my fantastic mum,
Otherwise you'll get a smacked bum!
And I'm glad to have a great mum!

Lauren Read (10)

World's Best Dad!

A dad is a person who's loving and kind,
And often he knows what you have on your mind.
He's someone who listens, suggests and defends . . .
A dad can be one of your very best friends!
He's proud of your success but when things go wrong,
A dad can be patient, helpful and strong.
In all that you do a dad's love plays a part
There's always a place for him deep in your heart.
And each year that passes, you're even more glad,
More grateful and proud
Just to call him your dad.

Khayroon Suleyman (10)

My Dazzling Daddy!

What is my dad like? Well . . .

Dad loves his Mercs,
To his Mercs he makes a few twerks,
He wants his cars to be the best,
Better than the rest!

He is always building extensions to our house,
Before it used to be the size of a mouse,
Ladies call my dad honey,
They think he has a lot of money!

Dad thinks that he is a chick magnet,
But Mum thinks that he is a fridge magnet,
He looks in the mirror and questions why he's so hot,
But some people think he's not!

Well I love my dad,
He is not mad,
He is not a baddie,
He is my dazzling daddy!

I love you, Dad!

Mandeep Hayer (11)

Why Can't Everyone Be Like My Mum?

My mum is the best mum ever
She is ever so clever,
She gets things for me
She even gets me my tea,
I'll always love her
She is my mother,
I came from her tum
And she is my mum,
Seeing her at the kitchen sink
It made me start to think,
Why can't everyone be like my mum?

Flora Maycock (10)

Mummy Is My Favourite Person!

I love my mummy so, so, ever so much
She's kind, she's wonderful and she helps me an awful lot
I love my mummy so, so, ever so much
She goes crazy and it makes me laugh until she stops
I love my mummy so, so, ever so much
We dance around together until the music stops
I love my mummy so, so, ever so much
We have a great time together until the music stops
I love my mummy so, so, ever so much
We have a great time together and enjoy ourselves 100%, yeah!
I love my mummy so, so, ever so much
We sneak things together and have lots of fun
I love my mummy so, so, ever so much
We snuggle up together every day
I love my mummy so, so, ever so much
I help Mummy every day
I love my mummy so, so, ever so much
We work together and have lots of fun
I love my mummy so, so, ever so much
I love my mummy so, so, ever so much.

Ashlin Watts (10)

Mummy

If all the mummies in the world were asked to stand in line,
the one who'd stand out as the best would definitely be mine!

My mummy makes the world go round, in my mind that is,
and when she's feeling really down, there's only one thing I can give,
a great big hug then spin her round, just like a merry-go-round
I'll think of something nice to say and that just makes her smile all day.

In all my heart I wish her well and hope your favourite is your mum
as well, but now it's time to say goodbye and leave this poem right behind I'll
treasure forever day after day, so now my question is . . .

      What's your favourite thing today?

Tamara Elms (11)

Love

My favourite person is my mum,
She smart and modest and lots of fun,
She is the dearest, she is the best,
And do you know why?
Love fills up her chest!

She makes my breakfast,
She prepares me lunch,
She cooks me dinner,
And sometimes brunch.

My favourite person is my mummy,
The food she cooks is always yummy,
She loves music and so do I,
And we both have problems with our eyes!

My mummy is the best to have,
She is the nicest without a doubt,
My mummy she is always funny,
And that is why:
I love my mummy!

Imogen Walsh (10)

My Favourite Person

My favourite person
is always there for me,
and I'm there for her.
Her name is Jess,
and she never makes a mess.
We have a lot in common,
we even have the same cars -
but we can tell them apart.
When she's down,
I'll cheer her up, somehow.
She is my best friend,
Jess - she's the best.

Zoe Straw (10)

My Best Dog, Lulu

My best friend is my dog, she is two years old.
She is very gentle, brave and bold.
She cheers me up when I am sad,
I give her cuddles when she has been bad.
She likes to sing to my guitar,
her voice goes, *'Ahh, ahh, ahh!'*
She fetches and carries when I throw her ball,
and comes straight back when I call.
She likes to eat anything from ice cream cones
to her yummy bones.
She likes to sleep with me at night,
and does not wake up until the sun is bright.
She loves to roll over and I tickle her tummy,
she makes me laugh because she is very funny.
She makes me feel safe and very protected
in her own special way,
I am so glad that I spend time with her each and every day.
I love and adore her,
that is why she is my best friend, *Lulu!*

Sophie Francis (10)

My Mum

My favourite person in the world would have to be my mum,
even when I'm naughty, she will never smack my bum.
She may have to send me to my room or shout at me a little,
but in the end we'll turn around and have a laugh and tickle.

She's always there in times of need and cares for me so much,
she knows all the different types of ways to give a mother's touch.

My favourite person in the world would have to be my mum,
we run around the living room having lots of fun.
From painting nails to makeovers and lots of jewellery-making,
Cookies, muffins, cakes and more, we make them when we're baking.

So my favourite person in the world will always be my mum.

Chloe Tamara Johnson (11)

My Favourite Person – Best Friend

It was a cold wintry day
When Debra and I went out to play
We met a dog at our local park
That stood famished at the oak tree bark
We decided to move far away
But the dog looked and decided to stay
We threw our balls from left to right
The dog ran so we flinched real tight
It got Debra and gnawed into her leg
'Help me please!' Debra begged
I was so frightened I couldn't help.
After the dog had gnawed into her bone
She lay helpless and began to groan
Later that day the ambulance came and took her away
I couldn't help so I waited and prayed.
Later I found out that she was disabled
I ran back home and told my mum, Mabel
The things I've seen have made me blind
But my best friend has left these things behind.

Veronica Faluyi (11)

My Teddy

My favourite person is my teddy called Freddie,
He has only got one leggie,
He's been my friend for years and years,
I like to bite his ears,

He's now rather dirty after years of play,
My sisters tells me, 'Throw him away!'

I cannot part with my favourite friend,
My Freddie, my Freddie,
My friend till the end.

I love you dearly with all my heart,
Me and you will never ever part.

Jack Greaves (9)

My Dog Luckie

My dog Luckie is 13 years old.
He's a cheerful chap with stories to be told.
He once stole my mum's tights and left them in the garden.
The postman came along and said, 'Oh pardon!'
Another time he ran away on a dull and dreary day.
He jumped the fence 6ft high,
To the shock of the neighbours passing by.
They could not believe what they had seen.
My dog was like jumping bean!
He likes to go out for long walks,
Through the fields and by the lochs.
Once we were out walking,
He chased the swans and it was shocking.
Swimming through the water as fast as he could,
The swans flew away into the nearby woods.
Passers-by stared in awe
As my dog came out with a muddy paw.
My dog is naughty and silly too,
But I love him lots and so would you!

Amy Parker (10)

My Favourite Person

My favourite person
has brown curly hair
does sport every day
and learns from morning to night

My favourite person
has trophies lying on his shelves
staring at me like they are mine

My favourite person
has two cool brothers
that annoy him twenty-four seven

My favourite person is my best friend, Jamie.

Declan Ingledew (11)

Untitled

My furry, fantastic dog Dennis,
You could call him a menace,
He's my favourite animal,
A fantastic mammal,
My loveable dog is a black Labrador,
That makes me love him even more!

I take him for a walk,
He is worn out when we've been,
Obviously he can't talk,
But I know he's very keen,
Where there's food about his eyes are like a hawk,
A dropped crisp or crumb would rarely go unseen.

He's always there for a cuddle and a treat,
His dog biscuits taste of beefy meat,
He's a part of our family and we all really care,
My mum hoovers up his hair,
She swears it will never end,
But Dennis, my cheeky, lazy dog, is my very best friend!

Sarah Titterington (12)

My Friend (Neave) Niamh

My friend Niamh comes down to play,
We don't stop till the end of the day.
We sing and dance in our fancy pants.
We jump up high till we touch the sky!
Let's do some more and get on the dance floor,
Boogie to the left then boogie to the right,
Come on Niamh, let's boogie all night!
Jump around and touch the ground,
There are some new moves to be found.
If you need to learn some more,
Just call Katie and Niamh onto the dance floor.

My favourite person is my cousin Niamh!

Katie McComiskey (6)

A Secret Smile

A smile is so special – but not just from anyone
My favourite person Megan gives a great smile
To keep me grinning on.
A smile of hers is definitely worthwhile!

We talk for lots of hours
And many minutes pass
With secrets, gossip, who loves who?
To make us giggle and laugh.

At school we have lots of fun
Working together we go far
On subjects like maths and literacy
As we gaze upon a star.

We do our secret handshake
Every day before school
And promise we will never
Ever break friends
Cool!

Ella Seaborn (10)

My Mum

My mum is like a best friend.
Always there for me she hugs me
Never bugs me, always sticks up for me.
I love my mum, she loves me too
She will always do so.
She never lets me feel alone.
I respect my mum so much,
That people think I'm dumb.
I don't care because my mum's there.
From the beginning all the way to the end.
If I cry she ends up crying too.
She helps me when I need help
Because we love each other.

Zara Kauser (11)

Wizzy Is The Best, Better Than The Rest!

Wizzy is my cat that loves to eat,
it used to be Felix,
but now she has biscuits and treats.

Wizzy plays with a lot of things,
ball, feathers, laces,
toy mice and Scooby strings!

Wizzy is black and white,
long whiskers, panda eyes,
and what a pretty sight!

When we play together,
(with a string) she nearly does flips,
I will always love her forever.

She is an indoor cat,
The closest she'll be to a front door
is on the inside mat!

Wizzy is the best, better than the rest!

Nicola Jeffs (11)

My Dad

My dad watches Simpsons with me
Our favourite person is Bart
Also my dad is very smart
He cuddles me at night
So that the nasty creatures don't bite
We are a fan of Spurs
And he makes me laugh by doing cats' purrs
We play on our Wii
He always beats me
Me and my dad eat chocolate ice cream
Also he tickles me until I scream
He is kind
But best of all he is all mine.

Jasmine Lauren Hope (8)

My Sugarfied Brother

My sugarfied brother likes all things sweet,
and makes me giggle when he has something to eat.
He likes sugar on Sugar Puffs and sweet cups of tea
which make him do a little wee.
I laugh at him sometimes and say, 'Your teeth will fall out!'
but all he does is scream and shout!
I really do wonder sometimes why he has twenty biscuits a day,
the shopping price goes up that my mum has to pay!
I don't know how my brother would live without sweets,
but I know he'd easily live without fruits, vegetables and meats!
His best treasure is the biscuit tin
and I think soon I'll need to pop him with a pin.
He likes cherry bakewells and a nice jam tart
and he also likes chocolate cake with which he will never part.
One of his favourites are lollipops all shiny and bright,
he also likes the fizzy drink named Sprite.
I couldn't name all the things my brother has eaten over the past seven years.
So now you know who the sugar king is, and that's my sugarfied brother!

Millie Cresdee (10)

My Fluffy Friend

My dog is bonkers
My dog is my friend
My dog is a game that never seems to end!

My dog likes to eat
She also likes to bark
My dog has pretty eyes that always seem to spark!

My dog is soft
She's also very waily
I don't know, maybe she doesn't like the name Daisy!

But most of all, my dog is loved
Not just by me, Dad, my brother and Mum
But by everyone.

Eloise Hillier (10)

My Grandad

I've got the most fantastic family.
My mum, my dad, my brother,
My poppa, two nannas and me.
We all have good times together,
They are all my best friends you see.
But there's one that I love
My own special friend.
Sadly he is no longer here.
He brought me sunshine when it was cloudy,
He brought me fun each day of the year.
I loved my grandad oh, so much,
His memory always brings a tear.
But his memory also makes me happy,
For I always know that he is near.
Guiding me, watching over me
Whilst I'm at school or out at play,
No matter where I am, or what I am doing,
He's with me every day.

Eleanor Gladman (11)

My Favourite Person

My favourite person is myself.
I am always kind to everyone else.
I love myself.
I am confident and intelligent.
I encourage others to be themselves.
Nobody can be you.
You are who makes you.
If you're not comfortable in your skin.
Whose skin are you going to be comfortable in?
I am comfortable in mine!
That's why I write these rhymes!
My favourite person is me!
Who else is it going to be?

Chardonae Stephenson (11)

My Best Sister

My sister is the best,
The best of the rest,
So many reasons why,
But here are just a few of them,
She's funny, talented and brainy
However she can be a bit lazy,
I don't mind that though,
She'll never be my foe,
She lets me stay up late,
That I'll never hate,
My sister is also really loveable,
And the jokes she makes are never dull,
When it comes to music,
She would get a big tick,
As I said before,
There are so many reasons more,
I like those the most,
Because with my sister I can always boast!

Suzie Frith (11)

Who Am I?

Who am I?
Tiny cutie
Fluffy baby
Gorgeous girlie
Little sweetie
Total veggie
Greedy eater
Golden-hearted
Totally trustworthy
Loyal friend
Who am I?
Chocolate the guinea pig,
Queen of my heart.

Katherine Stanley (9)

My Favourite Person

    M am, you are the best,
    Y ou're just like a shining star

    F avourite person, yes you are
    A nd you're there for me when I'm sad
    V ery special, yes you are
    O K I know my poem is bad
Yo U   make me happy when I'm sad
    R emembering memories that we have had
    I nviting friends round for tea
    T ogether we always laugh or cry
    E veryone can see how much you mean to me

    P rotecting me when things go wrong
    E very day I love you more
    R ecovering injuries together with me
    S o we love each other even more
    O n the ball you prance about
    N ow I love you more and more.

Abbie Weatherill (10)

Friendship

This poem is about . . .
 F un we have together
 R unning up and down the schoolyard
 I sabel is her name
 E very day we stick together
 N othing can break us apart
 D ay after day we are friends.

Isabel is my friend,
Our friendship will never end
It will be me and her all the time
We will never start a crime
We have our friendship tree
We go to each other's house for tea!

Charlie Taylor (9)

My Puppy

My favourite animal is my dog
he loves to play with me
he chews my socks and eats a lot
and is always friendly to me.

My puppy's name is Henry
but Hoover might be right
because my darling puppy
eats everything in sight.

He's black and white and gorgeous
he means the world to me
and is the latest member
of our happy family.

I love to walk my puppy
and play with him a lot
he was the greatest present
I think I ever got.

Meadhbh Murphy (11)

My Brother, Will

My brother is a minx
and he always stinks.
He can crawl
to the mall.
While he has a laugh
I'll send him to the bath.
His clothes are so cute
he likes to boot.
He likes his swing
I like to fling.
His smile is so lovely
and he isn't a bully.
He is so bright
he enjoys the light!

Holly Bate (6)

I Love My Mum

My mum is the best mum!
My mum is the greatest mum!
My mum is a fun mum!
But my mum is my mum!

I've got a friend called Baren,
It's funny because my mum's name's Karen
She's really 43
But she's just like me.

My mum's a bit like me.
She's the bee's knees.
We both like cheese
I guess she's a lot like me.

I love my mum
Mum loves me.
We're just like twins . . .
To me!

Hannah Sawitzki (11)

Family Of Fun

My favourite person, just what can I say?
They make me smile day after day.
I see them here, I see them there,
They're not invisible because they don't disappear.
My mum, my grandma, they're really nice, I wouldn't let them go, even for a million pounds, that has been given to me twice.
My dad, my uncle, they're both really clever,
I love them to bits, even more than my jacket made of leather.
My brother, my cousin, they're really cheeky,
without them my life would be geeky.
My aunty, my grandad, they're really funny,
They give me great hugs, that are sweet like honey.
So there you have it, my family of fun,
But to tell you the truth, I don't have a favourite one!

Visha Arfan (12)

My Fun, Furry Friend

My fun, furry friend,
On the sofa she is sat.
My fun, furry friend,
I must add she's a cat.

My fun, furry friend,
Running all around.
My fun, furry friend,
Leaping off the ground.

My fun, furry friend,
Catching mice all day.
My fun, furry friend,
Loves to jump and play.

My fun, furry friend,
On the sofa she is sat.
My favourite person in the world,
And she's my pussy cat!

Sacha Davies (11)

My Favourite Pet Named Cindy

My favourite pet's called Cindy
Although she's rather windy,
She likes to chase mice
Which isn't very nice,
When she can't be bothered to chase the mouse
She just sits around the house,
When the days are hazy
She always feels rather lazy,
Cindy was born in May
But now she's old and grey,
She used to be black,
Her collar is pink
So what do you think?
My pet's name is Cindy.

Faye McDonald (8)

Tia-Amor

Tia-Amor is my niece
Who loves to play princess
If I will play the prince
With long, blonde, curly hair
She really is the part.

Tia-Amor is a clever girl
Who always makes me laugh
With her cheeky grin
And her big blue eyes
She always makes me smile.

Tia-Amor is lots of fun
Who never stops talking
And dancing around the room
In her princess dress
She lights up all around her.

Tia-Amor, my niece.

Caleb Kennelly (11)

My Best Friend

My best friend has chickenpox,
I don't think she likes it lots.
We were supposed to go out and play,
But our mums said, 'Sorry not today.'
On Friday she will miss our school trip,
Now I will probably sit next to some boy drip.
Going to school is normally fun
But without Bryonie, I will be glum.
At playtime I suppose I'll cope
And try my best not to mope.
Now our gang won't be complete
Can't wait till she is better and back on her feet.
My best friend has chickenpox,
I don't think she likes it lots.

Mai Tumber (9)

The Early Deliverer

In the morning comes a man, wearing red all over,
Delivering letters everywhere: London, Swansea, Dover!
Rainy, sunny, cloudy, windy - comes whatever the weather,
If you think he's gonna be late . . . *No, not him, not ever!*

Junk mail arrives (that's important too),
Half price sales, from Hotters' shoes.
Christmas offers, still months to go,
Takeaway leaflets, eat in or to go!

Birthdays, postcards, young lovers wed,
The excited suspicion never ends.
Bills don't do the parents proud,
Barclays, Natwest all around!

Voting polls for God knows what!
Choosing strangers such and such.
Sky and Virgin info packs.
His shift's now over and that's that!

La'Raib Kamran Wayn (11)

My Favourite Person

My favourite person's very kind,
She's also generous you'll find.
She gives me 3 square meals a day;
I am a pampered pet you say!
She gives me squeaky balls and string,
And my favourite squidgy, chewy thing.
She lets me slink around the house.
Searching for a hidden mouse.
She strokes me with great affection
And cuts my fur to shimmering perfection.
She gives me such a comfy basket
Which gives me such pleasure I cannot mask it.
The best owner of any cat,
She's my favourite person and that is that.

Sam Jones (12)

The Catherine Tate Poem

I wander here, lonely as a cloud
Without millions of fans 'round me hovered
No more autograph-seeking crowds
And I pause to ask: 'Am I bothered?'

With my pure red hair hanging
I walk calmly in the summer breeze
I'm not now a schoolgirl ganging
And I'm not hunting alien bees.

I've experienced lots, loads, as such
From old age and monsters that scratch
I never get frustrated much
And anyway, there's not that much to catch.

I come by different names global
From Lauren to Nana to mate
Don't forget the cheeky Donna Noble
But you can just call me Catherine Tate.

Matthew Robinson (10)

Zara Philips

My favourite person rides a horse,
You'll find her jumping around the course,
Zara Phillips is her name,
Riding horses is her game,
When she competes she tries to win,
This sends the other riders in a spin,
Lots of rosettes she has won,
But the best bit about her, is she has fun,
She always looks after her horses well,
By just looking at them you can tell,
Falling off, she does that a lot,
But she gets back on and has a trot,
She's hardworking and very brave,
That's what makes her my fave!

Charlotte Williams (11)

My Best Friend, Emily

Emily is sweet, clever and cool,
She really pays attention at school,
She never moans and groans or cries,
She never even ever lies!

Emily is the best friend anyone could have,
She always tries to make you laugh,
Sometimes her laughing techniques don't work,
But I could never say she's a jerk!

She really does try to work things out,
She is the ultimate friend, no doubt,
Like I said, she's really cool,
One thing for definite, she doesn't drool!

Even if you and I tried,
This really is not a lie,
You couldn't find a friend better than her,
She's better than gold, frankincense and myrrh!

Sian Matthew (11)

My Brother

A brother is like a cheerful monkey.
A brother is like a non-stop chatterbox.
A brother is like a cuddly, soft bear.
That is like my brother.

A brother is someone who takes care of you.
A brother is someone who makes you smile every day.
A brother is someone who cheers you up in every problem.
A brother is someone who loves you every day.
A brother we have, isn't like a cat or dog.
    That someone is my delicate brother.

    My brother
      is the
        best!

Alisha Pandya (10)

My Favourite Person

He's fluffy and furry,
My best friend,
Hunts down prey with a mask of fury,
Together till the end!

Agile and superfast,
They're the words,
He jumps as high as an electricity mast,
His relatives can take down wildebeest in herds!

Snoozing and snoring,
In *my* bed,
Sometimes he's pretty boring,
Then he pulls an adoring face and tilts his head.

Charming in every way,
A+ in every 'best friend' test,
The person I chose was my cat!
So my cat's my favourite person.

William Fedorov (10)

My Secret Sam

Secret Sam is my horse
We ride in the school
Round and round
Until it is time for the swimming pool.

When we have ridden twice a day
I take him to the field to play
As soon as I shut the gate
He's off down to the stream
And all of his friends will be waiting there.

What mischief they get up to
I will never know
But even so
He is still my Secret Sam.

Nathan Crane (11)

He's My Brother

He's my brother, fun and naughty,
With his friends he's very sporty.
Playing games and having fun,
Is his speciality and that's done.

Now comes his differences with me,
When we eat I'm very tidy.
Then comes brother like a mess,
While we're eating he'll never confess.

When I follow him he turns red,
And with a shout he has fled.
And then I go after him with a giggle,
As I pass the door he starts to go purple and wiggle.

Next month he's going to high school,
Because he has finished preschool.
After all I will always love him,
So that's the end with my big brother.

Mathangi Sritharan (9)

Dad, I Wanted To Tell You I Think - You're A Hero

When I was a baby, you would hold me in your arms.
I felt the love and kindness, keeping me safe from harm.
I would look up into your eyes, and all the love I would see.
How did I get so lucky, you were the dad chosen for me.
There is something special about a father and daughter's love.
Seems it was sent to me from some place up above.
Our love is everlasting, I just wanted you to know.
That you're my special hero, Dad
And I wanted to tell you so.

You're a *superhero* to me
I love you loads, Daddy.

Eleasha Tahnee Makin (11)

My Best Friend

A great friend,
A true friend,
A wonderfully new friend,
Together, forever, we'll be.

A sweet friend,
A proud friend,
A graciously loud friend,
How perfectly lovely is she.

A bright friend,
A kind friend,
An out-of-her-mind friend,
She's fantastically perfect to me.

A posh friend,
A sleek friend,
A truly unique friend,
She's as real as a real friend can be.

Charlotte Balls (11)

Silly Billy

You may think it's rather silly,
But my best friend is my puppy Billy.
He falls and slips all over the place
And leaves everything in a state.
He's my best mate.
He likes to take my family's socks,
Then my mum shouts at him to get him in his box.
He greets me at the door, when I have been away,
He licks my face and brings his ball so then we can play.
When my mum and I sit and talk,
Billy barks and barks till we take him for his walk.
And when everyone in the house is asleep,
Up the stairs and into my bed he creeps.

Kelsey Clifford (10)

Rosie

She isn't an ordinary cat,
She chases no fish or bird,
And whenever she wants company,
She is sure to be heard.

Rosie sleeps anywhere,
Her favourite place is a box,
And when Rosie goes to sleep,
She pretends to be a fox.

Little Rosie is black and white,
With a small pink nose,
She is very beautiful.
Just like a delicate rose.

Rosie is a lovely cat,
And is very special to me,
She just has that gentle touch,
But has never climbed a tree.

Rebecca Scaife (10)

My Mum

You might think my mum
Is just an average mum
But you're wrong, she has a heart
That is as pure as gold
With a sparkle in every smile.
When her magical, soft hand touches your face
A rush of love and happiness fills you up
Like a balloon filled with helium.
She has supported me from the day I was born
And will carry on till the day I die.
So now I have told you my poem,
You know how lucky I am
To have a mum so special as that.

Amy Chandler (10)

My Household

I'm gonna tell you about my household
They're the best in every way
They're funny, kind and awesome
And I'd just like to say . . .

My nan is fantastic
And loves drinking tea
She's forever doing crosswords
She's special to me!

My mum is the best
She's like no other
She's awesomely great
The greatest mother.

And then there is me
My life's not dull . . .
I love my mum and nan so much
I'm *very* grateful!

Elllah Jackson (10)

My Favourite Person

My favourite person is brainy
My favourite person is smart
My favourite person has lots of friends
And one ginormous heart
My favourite person is gorgeous
My favourite person is sweet
My favourite person is someone
I bet you can't wait to meet
My favourite person is someone
In the mirror I always see
Have you guessed it?
I bet you have
My favourite person is *me!*

Emily Dalton (10)

Mum

You think I'm growing up too fast,
I think I'm going too slow,
I think I know all I need to,
You think I have a long way to go,

I may think I'm always right,
You know that you always are,
You always want to be near me,
I always seem to want to go too far.

I may leave my room in a mess,
And you may nag me to clean,
You may disapprove of the boyfriends I have,
And I'll say that you're just being mean,

We may argue some of the time,
But we'll always make it up in the end,
Because I'm your daughter, your little girl,
You're my mum, and my best friend.

Maddy Matthews (15)

A Mum!

A mum is someone who cares for you
It's like a wish come true . . .
My mum's not a dream or fantasy
She's not something out of the blue!
She's a dependable source of comfort
She's my pillow when I fall
She's always eager to lend a hand
And support me when I call
From gurgles to smiles and to laughter
You have always been there for me to look after
Without you in my life there'd be an empty spot of disaster
You healed it and replaced it with happiness and pleasure
You are my favourite person forever!

Kainat Abed (11)

Cheeky Little Monkey!

Oh me and my brother
We have so much fun,
We run around and play
Until the day's done.

The cheeky little monkey
Oh we love him so,
And every time we see him
He just seems to grow.

He's a gorgeous little baby
Loves me, Mum and Dad,
He makes my heart flutter
Makes all of us glad.

So yes, he is cheeky
Little monkey, that's him,
But what is so strong
Is the love from within.

Amy Jones (10)

My Favourite Person Is

If allowed I would choose 3 because we are a unit
Nan, Grandad, Snowy the cat and me.
Nan does everything for me, gives me hugs and kisses
When I'm not well lots of love I can tell.
Grandad takes me fishing,
Rides in the car more like my dad not grandpa!
Snowy chases about, makes me smile
Sits on my lap, purrs, plays chase and hides all the while.
This is a good life because of my unit filled with love and fun
Makes me know I'm the lucky one
I feel for the children who don't get the above,
Fun, laughter, food, love, warmth and care
It's what I hope one day they will share.

Kieran Morton (11)

I Have The Best Friend!

I have the best friend in the world
I have the best friend in the world
He is really important to me
He is really important to me

My friend is nice and cool
My friend is good at football
My friend is nice and helpful
My friend is good at running

I have the best friend in the world
I have the best friend in the world
He is really important to me
He is really important to me

My friend is nice and kind
My friend is good at basketball
My friend is nice and funny
My friend is good at tennis.

Ahmed Mohammed (10)

Harry Potter

If I had to choose
Harry Potter wouldn't lose,
Even though he's a character from a book,
He's not a pirate like Captain Hook.
He has a magic wand,
And a bond
To Ron and Hermione,
His friends. Can't you see?
His black hair conceals a scar
Which gives him powers to know if Voldemort is -
Near or far.
So I hope you see,
Why Harry Potter is for me!

Sophie Hannah Rowberry (11)

My Nutty Nan

All nans are special in their own way
But my nutty nan is terrific every day
She's crazy, she's cool, she's not your typical nan
And guess what? You'll never believe - she's a Chelsea football fan!

She has pink highlights and wears skinny jeans
And she never makes me eat horrible green beans
She always puts sugar in my tea
And at breakfast time she serves toast and salami.

She's really proud of me and always tells me so
And even when I'm really naughty she never tells me to go
She's the best, she makes me laugh, she's really funny
And I would never give her away for any amount of money.

She always buys me vanilla ice cream at the park
She even tries to ride my bike and often makes the dogs bark
That's my nutty nan, I have nothing else to say
Except I will always love her in every kind of way.

Felicia Martino (8)

My Little Brother

My little brother, Thomas,
Is really very sweet,
He captured my heart,
With his tiny baby feet.

When Mum and Dad are sleeping,
He really comes alive,
He becomes a little monster,
And that's before he's five.

When he was a baby,
He was a little bundle of joy
But that went out the window
When he grew to a little boy.

Zoe Holloway (10)

Biggest Fan

'Billie Jean' is my favourite
of all the songs he sang
I sing it all the time now
I think I'm his biggest fan

Very strange at first, I thought
because of the way he looked
then I learnt all about him
even bought a book

I discovered how talented he was
loads of amazing songs
then I listened all the time
all day and all night long

Although I never met him
I really miss him now he's gone
But Michael Jackson is my hero
And will be my whole life long!

Hollie Hopkisson (9)

My Favourite Person

My favourite person is my mum
She means the world to me
She's fun and playful all the time
And she makes a great cup of tea

She knows when I'm feeling down
She knows when I need a hug
She will make me laugh, being a clown
It doesn't matter if I'm bad or good

I love my mum with all my heart
And I know she'll always care
We will never ever be apart
Because in my mind she'll always be there.

Thomas Atherton (11)

My Favourite Person Is . . . God

I have lots of favourite people,
Who help me every day,
They teach me to love, learn and laugh
In every single way.

Mum loves and cares for me,
And Dad makes me laugh out loud with glee,
My best friends, Katie and Bethan, are crazy and weird,
But my old Grandad Stanhope is growing out a beard.

I have lots of teachers every year,
Some are so old, they've taught my peers,
But nobody could be as nice,
As the one and only Mrs Price.

But there is somebody I haven't mentioned yet,
He helps me when I get upset
And lives in the heavens up above,
My favourite person is God 'cause he's good and full of love.

Lucy Stanhope (11)

My Marvellous Mum!

I've written this poem about my mum,
Because she is so much fun.
She's there when I'm down,
She's like the ruler of my happy town.

I have to tell you my mum is very sporty,
She'll still be sporty when she's forty.
She shares her horse with me,
Mum teaches me to horse ride, you see.

She ran the Race for Life with her three sisters,
Luckily for Mum she didn't get any blisters.
Now you've read my poem about my mum,
I'm sure you'll agree she is so much fun.

Olivia Jarvis (11)

My Best Friend

I don't live near my best friend
So she's a treasure to see
Always making little knick-knacks,
Especially for me

She always seems to make me smile
The sun is in the sky
We know what's right for each other
So we never cry.

We have the same interests, a lot in common
We both run around.
We have sleepovers all the time
Where one of us makes a scary sound.

She is a friend never to forget
One to keep always
We'll both be looking after each other
For the rest of our days.

Ruby Crowhurst (11)

My Mum

I love you, Mum
you're so much fun,
you're kind and caring,
I always love what you're wearing.

You're always there for me
you cook my tea,
I spend your money
but you still call me Honey.

You're always cleaning
and you always know how I'm feeling,
on rainy and sunny days
I will love you always.

Charlotte Preece (12)

Why, Hannah?

Why? Why out of all the people in the world would I choose my little sister, Hannah? Well, here's why . . .

She's the sweetest little thing really, underneath all the tantrums and crying fits! But if you get to know her properly like I do, you'll find she is actually the greatest person you are ever likely to meet!

Hannah is only four, and yet she understands anything that you say. You can tell her anything and she knows exactly how you feel - strange really!

The best thing about Hannah is that she is my sister! We have lots of fun together; for example, we go on picnics together at the park, and have ice creams on the beach. Wherever we go she always manages to turn it into one big adventure!

Hannah - I love her, I kiss her, I cuddle her and most of all, I love to hug her!

Hannah, my sister!

Holly Marie Port (11)

Sean

My favourite person is my brother Sean
I have loved him ever since he was born

I love my brother Sean the most
And when we eat breakfast he nicks all my toast

He likes to be outside, wild and free
We like spending time together, just him and me

I think Sean is very cool
I miss him very much when I'm playing at school

Sean isn't good at spelling
But he is very good at yelling

My little brother is only just two
I love him loads and he loves me too!

Rebecca Ann Rigby (10)

All You Are

You're irreplaceable,
You're unbelievable,
You're inspirational,
You're phenomenal,
You're remarkable,
You're wonderful,
You're successful,
You're loveable,
You're peaceful,
You're blissful,
You're truthful,
You're grateful,
You're hopeful,
You're unforgettable,
And so memorable,
You're my mother, teacher and protector,
Yet for all you are only human and never far away.

Ruhi Ur-Rashid (14)

Mum

When I'm ill who cares for me?
My mum
When I'm feeling down who do I go to?
My mum

Who makes me my breakfast, lunch and dinner?
My mum
Who buys me clothes and shoes?
My mum

Who tidies up after me and washes my clothes?
My mum
Who helps me achieve my goals and ambitions?
My mum

        Thank you Mum!

Katy Strong (11)

She's Mine

My favourite person every day,
makes my problems go away.
She's beautiful and pretty,
very clever and witty.
She can be moody but I don't care,
because she's like my cuddly bear.
She's like a fairy in the sky,
always dancing and singing me lullabies.
The smile on her face,
lights up our place.
She picks me up when I fall,
then makes me feel strong and tall.
She's next to me under a willow,
lying with me on a pillow.
I cuddle her every day.
Love her in every way.
And that's my mum!

Abbie Storer (8)

My Dog, My Dog

My dog, my dog, my best mate,
Cuddly and cute, that makes him so great!
He's funny and furry and very, very clever,
He does tricks like roll over forever and ever.

My dog, my dog, my naughty, naughty dog
Gets away with licking my face
And hiding my shoes which gets me told off.

My dog, my dog, I love him so much,
He chases the cat then the rabbit around his hutch,
My dog, my dog, my funny, funny dog,
The laziest, dirtiest fleabag
In the whole wide world.

But I love him so much!

Amy Smith (9)

My Favourite Person

Brothers, brothers, oh brother . . . !
Funny, loving, messy and clever,
I could never replace him or wish for another.

Simple . . . simple!
Would describe him just right,
Nothing annoying apart from his
Unsleep-throughable snoozes by night.

Laughs and laughs - so hilariously amusing,
Pranking away like there's no tomorrow,
No sign or hint of regret or sorrow.

To sum up my brother to show he's the *best*
In a generous way: he's kind, thoughtful
And don't forget: all these things are the things
That can count; add up and you'll find just

Perfect!

Hannah Chow (11)

Untitled

Lucy's my dog
All fluffy and white
Makes me laugh all day and night
Jumps up on me and licks me to death
Makes me all soaking wet
I think of her as my big sis
Although she has one sloppy kiss
Tough for you, she is mine
And I will love her all the time

  A lfie is my dog
  L azy but a little rat
  F ighting all the time
  I see him in my right eye
  E ating all the cupcakes, but I love him all the time!

Dawn Claire Parsons (10)

My Favourite Furry Friend

Every time I call her name she comes,
Curiously looking around.
She will come and sit on my knee,
Purring louder than a car's engine.

She waits at the back door,
Trying to tell us that she wants to go outside.
Then after she has done her business,
She will pop up at the back door.

When she wants food, she strolls around the kitchen,
Looking at her empty bowl when she passes.
I feed her,
She looks at me as if to say, 'Thank you.'
Then gobbles it up.

She is a cat called Twinkle,
The best in the world!

Caitlin Burton (11)

My Special Friend

My special friend, intelligent, loyal and true,
In my sticky situations, I always think of you.
You are the very person with whom I share a bond,
I hope that you know that of you I am very fond.
You are that person that brings joy to my day,
Everything you have done for me, how can I ever repay?
You always cheer me up when I'm feeling blue,
Life would not be half as nice, if I did not have you.
When facing disappointment, heartbreak or pain,
I've been able to turn to you again and again.
You're like a sister to me, no wait, maybe more
With your good luck by my side I know I'll always score!
I want to repay you for the kindness you have shown,
As you're one of the greatest people I have ever known!
Thank you for being a special friend!

Maniba Kiani (11)

To You Mum

When times get hard and life too tough,
And things become a bit too much,
When stress and upset take a toll,
You step in with your motherly role.

Although you do it all alone,
You provide us with shelter and a cosy home.
You accept us for who we are,
Mum, you are our shining star.

You have been with us through thick and thin,
Making sure we don't give in.
You help to steer us in the right direction,
You show your love and affection.

So when you're sad or feeling glum
      Remember . . .
           We love you Mum!

Zoe Wilson (11)

My Brother

He likes to run about
He likes to jump about
He laughs and giggles
He's always in a pickle
He likes to jump about

He rolls around in mud
He jumps in dirty puddles
He likes to kick a ball
He always likes to win

He loves to ride his bike
He always wants to be in front
He likes to speed ahead
He loves to bump and shout
He is still my brother, I'd have no other.

Emily Lambourne (9)

Fluffy

Fluffy is my rabbit,
he is white and grey,
he never stops eating
and always loves to play!

I got him on my birthday in 2004,
I've had him five years now
but it certainly seems like more.

He's always very cheeky,
and hides when he is called,
he likes to stay in the garage
and leaves paw marks on the floor!

He loves to nibble Weetabix,
and lie down on the grass,
but when I'm in the sun lounger,
he just looks at me through the glass!

Alexandra Drysdale (11)

My Dad

My dad, he is special to me,
buying toys is where I want to be,
he walks round the shop
and helps me to choose.
In Toys 'R' Us you can never lose.

Games, puzzles, bikes and toys,
these are the things we like, us boys.
So many things to have fun with,
the choice is endless, I'm in a whizz.

Me and my dad are two of a kind,
building, making, playing at his age,
Never mind!
I love my dad, he means a lot,
at the till, I spend all the money he has got.

Adam Allaway (9)

My Mum

My mum is my hero,
My mum's made for fame,
My mum should win a trophy for the mum who saved the day,
My mum shows patience in *everything* I do,
Even if it is totally out of the blue,
If you have a question she'll answer it for you,
Even though it might not be the right answer too,
My mum doesn't know everything but it seems like that at times,
My mum is a superstar,
It's written in her eyes,
People always say to me, 'Oh, you look like your mum.'
And I know I'm very lucky to have her good looks,
Her hair is lovely,
Her brain is smart,
My mum is a superhero coming to the rescue
Wherever you are!

Kirsty Wishart (11)

My Niece, Molly

My niece is named Molly,
She is cute like a little dolly.
Molly is one year old,
She is worth a sack of gold.

My niece can be a terror,
But she's also very clever
Molly is normally very happy,
She makes smelly nappies.

My niece likes to play with phones
Molly gobbles up ice cream cones
I love Molly with all of my heart
I'd love to put her in a shopping cart.

That's why I'm certain
Molly is my favourite person.

Clayton Ryan (11)

She's Always There

My favourite person is my mummy,
She's very kind and sometimes funny.
She looks after me wherever I go,
No matter if it's in the sun or in the snow.
She takes away my worries too,
Making grey skies turn to blue.
When I get myself into a muddle,
She's always there to give me a cuddle.
If I fall over and scrape my knee,
She's always there saying, 'Oh, let me see.'
She has no time to treat herself,
She's always there thinking about everyone else.
My mum is the best, can't you see?
I love her and she loves me.
So next time when I'm feeling glum,
She'll always be there, *my mum!*

Shona Macdonald (11)

My Favourite Person!

My favourite person is an author
She is an award-winning woman
An amazing writer!
Can you guess who she is?

She has written about a girl
Who has a sister called Pearl
And maybe another about some twins
Can you guess who she is?

Her best book is about Tracy Beaker
Who is a trouble seeker
She is an author with a ring on every finger
Can you guess who she is?

My favourite person is . . .
                        Jacqueline Wilson!

Sajida Desai (10)

My Mum

My mum is the best, she's my favourite person
Better than all the rest
She's kind and nice
Always been there for me.
When I was five I did once cry
She knew just what to do
Kiss me on the head and hug me tight
The pain just went away
Now that I'm twelve
I'm big to small
Now that I'm 5 foot tall
My mum seems very small
But she loves me more and more
I'll wrap this up nice and neat
To finish off . . . 'You know my mum's the best,
Unlike all the rest!'

Jordan Moores (12)

I've Got A Cat!

My cat's named Tiger
He loves rats
Drinks his milk
And sits on mats.

Goes to sleep
Chews hats
Talks to kitten
And is scared of bats.

Sometimes shy
Scared of boys
He licks his fur
And plays with his toys.

I love my cat
And that's that!

Zara Khan (9)

My Mum

This poem is about someone I adore,
I'm sure as I speak you will love her more and more.
My start in life was mean and misunderstood,
But with her by my side I knew life would be good.
She showed me tricks old and new
Going through it loads of times until I finally knew what to do.
My past was misty and black,
Then I look at her and my life is back on track.
I'm lucky to have her by my side with a big smile I cannot hide.
I'm older now and can look after myself
But she does still wipe my mouth.
I may leave home, which means I will go,
But all the love and happiness I will still show.
I know that time will come,
But I will always say,
'I love you, Mum.'

Molly Faulkner (12)

My Favourite Person!

Mummy is my favourite person,
She's small, smart and sweet
She can be tough when things are rough
But overall she's neat.

Her eyes are sparkly green,
Her hair the colour of dragon's breath
Her growl is just as bad,
Which sometimes makes me sad
But only if I'm bad.

Mummy takes me places
Makes plans and sticks to them
She organises lots of things
To keep the family amused!

My mum is simply the best.

Rebekah Whitnell (11)

My Friend Niall

There's one person I know that makes me smile
He's my best friend and his name is Niall
He's the only one I know all about
And a person I could never live without
Because without Niall my life would be dull
It would be like being stuck in an eternal lull
I can always trust him to tell me what's right
Because we never argue or fight
Niall supports me at everything I do
And he's always there when I need him too
Niall is caring and kind
This is why to me he is close at mind
So everyone with friends out there
To help them learn, laugh and share
Be a friend to someone down
Help them lose and forget their frown.

Eoin Coulter (10)

Minnie Mouse

I went to Florida
And all my dreams came true
I met Minnie Mouse
And all her friends too

I went in her house
And sat on her chair
I loved her spotty red dress and bow in her hair
Minnie and Mickey made such a great pair

Her fur was so soft
And jet-black
I was so upset when we had to pack

Unfortunately dreams have to end
And we had no money left to spend
Hopefully one day we will meet again!

Emma Wagstaff (10)

My Brother Charlie

My brother Charlie is my favourite guy
Listen to this and you'll soon see why
My brother Charlie is nearly twelve years old
But thankfully he's not yet going bald
My brother Charlie is not very tall
But is fantastic at his favourite sport, football
My brother Charlie is going to high school in September
He might meet a friend of the opposite gender
My brother Charlie plays the guitar
And hopes one day he'll become a star
My brother Charlie plays on his Xbox all day long
But hates it when I try to sing him a song
My brother Charlie is really kind
When I go in his room he doesn't mind
My brother Charlie is really great
You'll want him to be your best mate.

Mathilda Bassnett (10)

Ruby Anne

My favourite person,
She always has a big smile on her face,
it's like she's in a race, and she just won first place.

My favourite person,
She's always looking pretty and colourful,
She's so colourful and bright,
She would make you lose half your eyesight.

My favourite person,
She always has a lot of energy,
She always wants to get up and run,
I wish she could, it would be so much fun.

My favourite person is little but funny
And she's the only one with a lovely name
And that's *Ruby Anne!*

Annie Smith (9)

Friendship

From the moment we met
Somehow I just knew
I've found a new friend
Who I can turn to
We sometimes get so busy
That we cannot make a fuss
About the ones we care for
And who mean so much to us
A friend is like a shady tree
Beside a summer way
A friend is like the sunshine
That makes a perfect day
A friend is like a flower
That's worn close to the heart
A friend is like a treasure
With which one will not part.

Mollie Nixon (8)

A Gift . . . My Big Sister

So graceful and sweet,
Perfect pointy feet,
Gold soft cheeks,
And a smile to die for.

A perfect spin,
And every time a win,
Her head held up so high,
So confident and unshy.

Like a beautiful, delicate butterfly,
Reaching for the sky,
Softly dancing across the stage,
Something to be proud of,
A gift sent from above, heavenly love,
My big sister!

Bianca Walker (15)

My Little Cat

My furry little furball cat,
As thin as a pancake.
Her blue squinty eyes,
Sparkle in the daylight
And as swift as a fox, in the night.

She goes in the dishwasher,
Licks our plates clean!
She goes in the oven
And nicks our roast dinner!
She is the worst mannered cat in the world!

I love the way she curls up in my bed,
Snuggles down and purrs like an engine.
The clock strikes nine
And oh no it's dinner time.
That little cat, we'll never forget you.

Brandon Dudley (11)

My Favourite Person In The World

I am blessed with the greatest mum one can have;
To love my mum with all my heart who also loves me.
Because of the gift of love my mum means everything to me,
My mum is my favourite person in the world.

My mum makes my world all that it is,
A much better place than it would be without her,
I can't imagine what it would be like if we weren't together.
Our love is the most precious thing in my life,
And is what I am most thankful for.
Yes I have lots of favourite things,
Favourite memories, favourite people.
But when it comes to the one who means most to me,
I hope it's no surprise to you
That my mum is my favourite person in the world.
I love my mum!

Faheema Shaikh (11)

My Friend Georgia!

M y friend Georgia is funny and kind.
Y ou would like to meet her.

F riends are the world to me.
R eal good friends who you can trust.
I n hard and easy times they're always there.
E ven if it's hard for them too.
N ever ever doubt a friend.
D on't give up on a friendship either.

G eorgia is the bestest friend ever.
E ven though she is very strange.
O r individual as I call it.
R eally happy all the time.
G eorgia is my bestest friend.
I n games and real life.
A lways there for me.

Lillian-Mae Nuttall (10)

My Mum

The most important job I know
Is caring for me as I grow
A job like no other
My mother
She will most certainly need
Very special talents indeed
Teacher, doctor
Advisor and ref
Must cook and clean
Paint, sew and be a chef
Absolute devotion is essential
As well as lots of hug potential
24 hours every day
With no time off and no pay

And that's why I love my mum!

Maria Chesnaye (10)

Having Fun With My Best Friend

(Dedicated to Laura Brookes)

My favourite person is my best friend,
'Cause there's never a bad situation,
With our friendship there will never be an end,
Because of our relation.

We've known each other since we were born,
And now we're still so close.
From time to time we have sworn,
We will stay together no matter what.

We've had never-ending sleepovers,
Sweets until we were sick!
But just us being together, has made me figure out
What life is all about . . .
                Having fun!

Bailey Corbett (9)

My Mam

My mam is so caring
She likes sharing!

My mam is so fun
And she still gets her jobs done.

Kisses and cuddles all day long
And even some song!

We play together
In nice weather.

She does things that I like to do
She likes dancing too.

Now it is time to go and play.
It's going to be a fantastic full-of-fun mega day!

Do you have lots of fun with your mam?

Anna McCoy (9)

Cassie Dog

My friend Cassie
Faithful lassie
Smiles a canine smile.
She'll always be a friend to me
I'll stroke her for a while.

I'm never alone
When she's at home
She always comes to me
Her shining eyes and wagging tail
Are always good to see.

I've never had a better friend
Throughout many years
I love her from her paws and tail
Right through to her ears.

James Allbrook (10)

My Little Sister!

My little sister's name is Avneet,
I can tell her all my secrets.
When my little sister cries
her nose is as red as a cherry tomato.

When I am upset and start to cry
my little sister cheers me up.
Little sisters are special.
You can do loads of things with them like play teachers.

Sisters are special,
sisters are fun!
My sister has loads of toys,
but who doesn't like to play with those *boys!*

My little sister is very special to me . . .

Amreena Kaur (11)

Who Is The Grandma?

Who is the grandma that lives by the sea?
Who is the grandma that brings us trays of tea?

Who is the grandma that missed my date of birth?
Who is the grandma that gives me lots of mirth?

Who is the grandma that comes into class?
Who is the grandma that likes cutting the grass?

Who is the grandma that snores at night?
Who is the grandma that hates heights?

Who is the grandma that has pink lips?
Who is the grandma that takes me on trips?

Who is the grandma that I love very much?
Who is the grandma that always keeps in touch?

Lily Temple (11)

My Special Mum

S   is for her splendidness, her pleasantness around the family.
H   is for her hard-working attitude, her intelligence and esteem.
O   is for her oriental brilliance because she glimmers like a star in the night sky.
R   is for her reliability, her resplendence and her respect.
U   is for her understanding personality, she cares for me with all her heart and soul.
F   is for her fantastic perfection and her delightful manner towards everyone she meets.
A   is for the admirable and grandiose person that she is.

Altogether, all of these marvellous features make up my truly outstanding . . . Mum!

Farhana Begum (10)

My Favourite Person

When I cry, you wipe my tears,
When I'm scared, you calm my fears,

You give me lots of hugs, so tight,
And tuck me in my bed at night,

You encourage me in all I do,
I know I mean the world to you,

You say to me, 'Sit up straight, like a plank of wood.'
Yes, it's annoying, but you do it for my own good,

You keep me dry and safe and warm,
And cuddle me if there's a storm,

I hope I turn out the way you want me to be,
So thank you Mum for being there for me.

Erin Scorgie (11)

My Favourite Person – Dad's Never Sad

My dad's never sad
but he can be very mad
telling me five times a day
'Make your bed, no time to play!'

My dad's never sad
luckily he can be glad
he says it's 'cause I make him smile
he also thinks that I'm fragile!

My dad's never sad
and he says that I can be bad
I love my dad in every way
and he loves me, that's what he says.

Lindsey McIlwaine (10)

My Rabbit Lily

I've only had her a week today
but now she's officially here to stay
I sometimes talk to her at night
and also stroke and hug her tight

She has creamy fur and cute little paws
she has big front teeth and she loves to gnaw
I love her big brown eyes and tiny ears
and in the morning from her hole, she appears

She loves to come out and play
and settles down at the end of the day
sometimes she's sneaky and clever
but after all, she's the best pet ever!

Leanna Bradbury (11)

Twice As Nice

Twice as nice
Twice the fun
More the trouble
Nothing to be done.

Double the laughs
Lots of cuddles
Mummy's always
In a muddle.

I love my twin sisters
Lots and lots
Even more than
Jelly Tots!

Sian Farai Chinamora (8)

My Grandad

My Grandad John always sings a song
And is always here for me
Nothing in the world could ever break our bond
Because he is so great you see.

Everything I need he does
I love him lots because he helps me with my work
And hugs me when I'm hurt

When bullies are mean
Grandad sets the scene
And he makes the bullies stop
He is just the greatest grandad
He is absolutely top of the pops!

Kraig Wymer-Webb (11)

My Favourite Person

The wonderful thing about Tigger,
Is that he's the only one,
He bounces, bounces, bounces, bounces
And bounces all day long.

I've had him since I was little,
I'm his biggest fan,
So if you see him
Tell him that I am.

He's the best pet in the world,
Tigger never needs to be fed,
I love to give him hugs
And tuck him into bed!

Ellie Bulloch (10)

My Mum

You are always there for me,
I've known you for so long,
You told me today that you loved me,
Now I feel I'm strong.

I know very much that I love you,
Because I'm so close to you,
In many ways you're more than a friend,
It's just the crazy things you do.

You are my favourite person,
On this entire Earth,
You're the person who helps me through,
And I will also love you too.

Bryan Letters (11)

My Number 1 Cousin

I can remember when you were born,
I was so excited.
All the fun times
We had eating out and playing.

I love the way you knock the door,
I know it's Jacob standing there.
When I hear you laughing
It brightens up my day.

All the happy memories,
The photos I've kept.
Although I hardly see you,
You will always be in my heart.

Nadine Foster (11)

My Favourite Person

My favourite person is my imaginary friend!
She is so clever she can even bend.
We go on her broomstick and fly so high.
She is a wizard so we can buy everything in the sky.

We go on adventures to ponds and lakes.
We even met a dragon called Fire Drake.
We rake up leaves in the local park,
While polishing some tree bark.

We saw a rabbit bouncing round.
And a sing-song bird tweeting on the ground!
My favourite person is my imaginary friend
Without her my world would end.

Annie Goulding (8)

My Best Friend

My best friend's name is Mollie
And her hair is strawberry-blonde
She has big brown eyes
And of her I'm very fond.

She has a cat called Snowflake
Who walks with her to school
She likes to bake chocolate cake
I think that's really cool.

We like to go to the beach
And swim in the sea
Then we eat a sandwich each
Before we go home for tea!

Alex Anna Mackay (7)

My Magnificent Mum

My mum is magnificent, she's filled with joy and love.
My mum is magnificent, she's as peaceful as a dove.
My mum is magical, she's always there to play.
My mum is magical, she's special in every way.

My mum is super, she is very kind.
My mum is super, she's always in my mind.
My mum is amazing, she is like a sweet.
My mum is amazing, she's a person you'd like to meet.

My mum isn't good, she's great.
My mum makes sure she is never late.
My mum is always fun.
My mum is #1.

Heather Addison (11)

My Favourite Person: James Patterson

All authors are really cool,
But James Patterson can top them all,
With brilliant stories and great titles
I'm sorry Dahl but move along!

It was really hard to choose one out of the rest,
But James Patterson simply is the best!
With brilliant stories and great titles,
Sorry Rowling but move along!

I know it's rude and all of that,
But all other authors need to learn that,
Patterson is better than them,
Sorry Rick Riordan but move along!

Joshua Andrew Foakes (10)

My Mum

(My favourite person)

Mum makes me laugh when I'm down,
She makes me smile when I frown,
Mum is always there, she will always care,
She treats me like I am an angel in the sky,
If I am upset, she will sort it out,
For Mum is always caring and sorting things out,
My mum is fantastic,
She's like elastic,
She always stretches to help,
If I'm down,
She picks me up off the ground.

Katrina Newlyn (10)

My Brother, Jack

My brother, Jack,
Always gives me flack,

I am seven, he is one,
He's very cheeky and lots of fun.

Mummy has her work cut out,
Cos Jack is always running about.

He makes me laugh,
He is so funny.
He always makes the weather sunny.

Bedtime comes, I give Jack a kiss,
My little brother I love to bits!

Tyler Parry (7)

My Favourite Mummy

Mummy's my favourite person in the world!
Because Mummy is caring and kind to animals,
Rescuing them when they are hurt.

Mummy's my favourite person in the world!
Because she cooks delicious dinners
Although they might not be to everyone else's taste.

Mummy's my favourite person in the world!
Because she likes to watch my girlie films
And eat popcorn.

Mummy - my favourite person in the world
Because I love her dearly and she's my mum!

Alicia Chapman (10)

Mummy

I look up to my bestest mum,
Like I look up to the stars.
Her smile is like the shiny moon,
That makes me feel all calm.
When she walks around the house,
She leaves behind a glow.
A glow full of life,
That she ties up with a bow.
Her hugs are really warming,
Although her hands are really cold.
She would probably be much nicer,
If I did what I was told!

Kassi Watson (11)

Finn

My baby brother makes me smile
He's not called John, Robert or Kyle
He has blue eyes, a dimple on his chin
He's called Big Brave Mighty Finn
He's brave ya see, and special to me
Even though he's annoying, helpless and wee
He has a battery in his heart
Cos the doctors in Yorkhill are very smart
It won't hold him back, he's really strong
I'll teach him what's right from wrong
I'll keep him safe every day
Teach him things and show him the way!

Cameron MacReady (9)

Wayne Rooney

My favourite person is Wayne Rooney,
he is the greatest, he is the best,
he's better than all the rest,
even though I've never met him,
he is still my favourite person,
with friends and family there to support him,
he is still an amazing person,
with people screaming and cheering
as he takes to the pitch,
with many goals that make him flick,
with 100 goals for Manchester United,
no wonder he's my favourite person.

Olivia Blanks (10)

A Dedication To Puddles

Puddles is my favourite calf, she is an Aberdeen Angus,
I love her very much.
She only comes up when she wants feeding,
Or when she's lonely.
She misses me when I go to school,
My daddy said I could keep her.
I miss her because she's in another field called the Flats,
I bet she misses me because I miss her.
She is six months old, I am eight,
Her mummy is three, her brother is one and a half.
Her daddy is seven.
I love Puddles and she loves me.

Niamh Walls (8)

My Daddy

My daddy is tough,
My daddy is sometimes rough,
And he likes to puff on a ciggy,
He eats like a piggy,
It may seem funny,
But he hasn't got much money,
It may not seem fair,
But he likes to brush his hair,
It may seem weird,
But he hasn't got a beard,
So I will always love him,
because he's my daddy.

Grace Hopkinson (11)

My Mum

My *mum* is always there for me when I have to take tablets
and when I'm in hospital with a drip in me, or something is wrong.
She makes me dinner and does loads for me.
I have cystic fibrosis so my mum runs around a lot.
She will never shout at me because she knows
I have a hard time with things.
I have a lot of tablets a day.
I also have asthma so she helps me a lot,
and when I get angry she calms me down,
by telling me to calm down about things,
and when I'm upset, she hugs me and kisses me,
and pats my back when I cough.

Aaron Vittles (11)

She's My Favourite Person

My favourite person's hair is blonde
She really likes seeing the real James Bond
He eyes are as green as the grass
She'll never miss out on any class
She loved Alton Towers, Oblivion she liked best
She never got down to sit, have rest
She works in the bank, what a lovely way
Of seeing the customers having to pay
I love her, she's my best friend
But sometimes she drives me round the bend!
It's my sister, the teenager, what can you say?
She's all grown up to this very day.

Liza Koroleva (11)

My Favourite Person

My favourite person is my mum,
She reminds me of the flavour in my chewing gum.
She takes me places everywhere,
Whenever I want her she's always there.
My mum is never terrible,
I love her so much I wish she was edible.
Any problem, any worry,
She's there in a hurry.
She takes care of me day and night,
She always keeps me very right.
She has loved me since I was as small as a dot,
She'll always be my mum no matter what.

Jamie Cooke (10)

My Cousin, Tallulah!

My cousin, Tallulah, is one year old,
She can scream and shout,
She's really very bold.

She plays with her toys all afternoon,
She makes loads of noise
And runs around the room.

She babbles and squeals
When she wants her meals,
She follows me round, it can get annoying,
But I love her all the same
Because she's my cousin, Tallulah.

Francesca Slattery (12)

Eloise, My Sister

My favourite person is not big at all,
but to be perfectly honest, she's not very small.
We've been through it all . . .
the big toothy grins,
the laughing, the shouting,
the unnecessary dins.

The measles, chickenpox,
the colds and all,
when I was big and she was small.

The squabbling, the fighting, the making friends,
It's a love and hate that never ends.

Holly Douch (10)

My Best Friend

My best friend is like me or you,
I met her when she was in Primary 2.

Linsey is my best friend's name
our personalities are about the same.

We are both mad and crazy,
but sometimes we can be lazy.

You could never make us part,
we've been friends from the start.

We do practically everything together
and I'm sure our friendship will last forever.

Lucy MacDonald (11)

Mum, My Favourite Person

You have the sweetest smile that there could ever be
and most of all I love you for always loving me.

Moon - sun - rainbow - flower
you are my superstar.

She tells me what is wrong - what is right
Listening to her always, my future is so bright.

If I'm in pain - she is caring
If I'm full of joy - she is sharing

        All the time
        She is so loving.

Malik Shahzad Khan (8)

My Favourite Person Is My Mum

My favourite person is my mum
because she plays with me.
My mum is my favourite person
because she helps me with my homework.
My mum is my favourite person
because she cooks my meals
My mum is my favourite person
because she is the best mum in the world
and that is why I love my mum.

*I love you
Mum!*

Katrina May (9)

My Mum

My mum, she's best, she's better than the rest,
She's kind and caring, loving too,
If I have a problem, she will always know what to do,
Each day she seems to get better and better,
You would think that, too, if you met her.

She sometimes seems a friend as well as a mum,
That's why she is such good fun,
If I have a sad frown upon my face,
She will put my smile back into place,
She's always on the ball, always switched on,
For a mum, I could not have asked for a better one.

Megan Hughes (11)

My Best Friend

It's good to have a special friend,
To talk to when I'm blue,
And life would not be half as nice,
If I did not have you.

You make me laugh and smile,
Whenever you're around,
We love to be together
What a special friend I've found!

Always together

Best friends forever!

Caitlyn Michelle Kirby (10)

Dad

You are the one
and only,
Without you I'd
be lonely,
If I didn't
have you,
I'd be so
sad,
Yes you are
my special
dad.

Benjamin Hartshorne (11)

My Pal, Kate

I guess it's fun having a mate,
But no one's pal is quite like Kate!
Your imagination goes wild when you think about her,
Because sometimes she roars yet sometimes she purrs.
Her mind is different to all others in a quite spectacular way,
She likes shortbread, yet she is tall,
But Tuesday is her favourite day,
She eats and sleeps, hums and snores,
So yet, she still is always adored,
And now I must confess,
Kate's my best friend, yes, the *best!*

Ella Turney (11)

About My Mum

I love my mummy
She is so funny
Her food is so yummy
When I am mad
I get so bad
My mummy says
'That is not funny!'
She will give me a hug
Make me feel loved
And that is what you call
A special mummy!

Ryan Brown (10)

Spike

You are the love in hearts.
You are the beat in beat it.
You are a he not a thing.
You make my heart pump.
You are the cables in the Wii.
You are the heat in a warm bath.
You are Heaven's light.
You are the shine from my teeth.
You are the excitement of Christmas.
You are the juice in grapes.
You are my favourite pet.

Mark Bell (9)

My Gran

My favourite is my gran,
you may call her Nan.
She's a super-duper cook
and she can still read a book.
Although she is quite old,
she can still mine for gold.
She wears glasses all the time,
and she still knows how to rhyme.
Remember that when you're old,
you don't always have to be bold
and now my story's all told.

Rhys Langley (9)

My Favourite Person

My favourite person is as clever as a mouse
And is always cleaning the house
She helps when I am sore
This person always has a special cure
This person loves me
And is always hurrying around
Like a busy bumblebee
I'm sure you will see
That she means the world to me
She is like no other
This person is my mother.

Rebecka Barwood (11)

Seren And Me

S eren is my favourite person.
E xcellent at swimming.
R ummages through her toys.
E xtremely fun.
N icely street dances.

A nd has a brother.
N ine in a couple of weeks.
D oes fantastic in gym.

M usic is so her thing.
E xcitedly goes to the beach.

Rhiannon Morgan (8)

He Is . . .

He is like the sunshine on a dark, rainy day
with his laughter.

He is always there for me
He is like my shadow.

He is my smile when I am sad.
He is upset when we are apart.
He is very special to me.
He is the best.
He is my brother, Oliver.
He is my favourite person.

Lauren Drysdale (11)

Stepsister

She is my lovely stepsister
She is also my best friend
We find each other annoying sometimes
But I always know I can depend on her.

No matter what the problem is
I know she will always be my best friend
She is a lovely person
Kind, thoughtful and honest.

I wouldn't be without her
And will always love her so.

Hannah Clarke (8)

Uncle John

Special Uncle John, sadly passed away
I vowed to remember him every night and day
Quite the card, he was a joker
He laughed at every joke,
He never failed to give you the giggles
He was quite a funny bloke

Uncle John is gone
He had many friends, and he was one of mine.

RIP Uncle John
(1948 - 2009)

Jack Riley (10)

My Dad

My dad is very funny,
even when he has a runny tummy.
Maybe he is 43,
but he will always play with me,
every day when I am bored,
or if it is something I can't afford,
he will do something for me,
sometimes it might be an ice cream.

Now that is what my dad is like to me,
so bye now, I am going to play with my dad, *yippee!*

Aaron Karn (11)

My Auntie Nicky

My auntie Nicky has blond hair
And goes through life without a care
She has colourful clothes and a very strange bag
You couldn't call her a 'footballer's wag'

She makes me smile when I am down
And makes me laugh when I frown
She collects angels, fairies and other strange things
And when the music's on, very loudly she sings!
In the holidays, I love to stop there
My auntie Nicky has blond hair.

Ryan Leatherland (9)

Granda, I Love You

Granda, I love you.
You work all day, you work all night.
You take me places that I want to go.
You take me to the beach so we can play and splash.
You take me to Auntie's
So I can play with my cousin.
You keep me safe, you keep me warm.
You make sure I'm OK.
You make sure I'm happy.

I *love* you, Granda.

Sydney Clay (9)

My Sister, Tash, Rocks

My sister, Tash, rocks
Even when she wears odd socks
She makes me laugh
And forces me to bath
My sis, Tash, rocks.

My sis, Tash, rocks
She taught me to read clocks
She forced me to the library
Now you can't find me
But my sis, Tash, still rocks!

Kristian Lacey (11)

Jordan Metcalfe Rocks

Jordan Metcalfe is my favourite TV star,
He'll definitely beat the rest by far,
He stars in Genie In The House,
Adil, the genie, he plays and he is no mouse,
He lives in a lamp at a house with the Nortons,
And used to live next door to the Horntons,
He grants Emma's and Sophie's wishes that are made,
He sometimes mucks them up but they will fade.

Jordan Metcalfe
Rocks!

Georgia Hunt (11)

Number 1 Mum

My favourite person is my mum.
I think she is number 1.
She cooks and cleans and washes the pots
And also ties very good knots.
She takes us everywhere
And buys us new underwear.
When we are feeling down
She picks us up off the ground.
There's nothing more to say
I love my mum, more and more every day.

Callum Donelan (11)

My Favourite Person

Gabrielle
  G ood or bad weather she still goes outside,
  A nd as she feels happy, her feelings stick to mine.
  B right is the sunlight on her face,
  R eflecting her magical smile.
  I n her eyes are stars twinkling, sparkling all the time
  E xcitement fills the air with fun,
  L ocking the boredom away,
  L eaving the joy and the memory saying:
  E veryone can play!

Rosa McManners (10)

Brown Bear

My favourite person is someone very close to my heart.
He may not be a person exactly but I still love him.
He's small and brown, soft and friendly.
I can tell him anything, my worries, my secrets, he'll never tell.
My favourite person is my teddy, Brown Bear.

Chloe Godding (11)

Mummy And Daddy

I love my mummy and daddy,
They care for me and love me,
They take me to school and pack my lunch,
And they always buy me a snack to munch,
When I am ill they care for me,
They share jokes and laugh with me,
They buy me chocolates and sweets,
And different types of treats.
I love my mummy and daddy,
And they love me too!

Anukiraha Uthayarajan (10)

My Favourite Person

Alfie is my dog. Alfie Dog to you,
his nickname, Alfie Walfie Wooo!
His favourite is a stick or ball
his worst nightmare, a shopping mall!
His fur is so fluffy while his eyes are dark brown
he is cowardly, far from a vicious hound!
But when he goes to bed the sun dies down
only for a few hours as soon he's up and alive!
So that's my Alfie, Alfie Dog to you
A white ninja in a car, Alfie Walfie Wooo!

George Stefan Acquaah (10)

Auntie Collette

My Auntie Collette, when she bakes
it makes you feel great,
the smell goes round your heart,
it tastes so fine, it is divine,
this is why I love my Auntie Collette.

Demi Allan (10)

My Mum

My favourite person is my mum
But sometimes she thinks I'm a pain in the bum.
With my mum, what can you say?
I practically get my own way
My mum works hard every day
Mostly in Wales, near the bay
On the market to sell her beds
Also headboards in blacks and reds
I love my mum and she loves me
She is the flower and I am the bee.

Holly Neary-King (10)

Jack

Oh what a mate
I think he's great,
When I play with Jack
The sky is never black,
The leaves are always green
When with Jack I'm seen,
If I was true to my heart
We would never be apart,
But Jack may move away
Yet my heart will never stray.

Katie Button-Williams (11)

My Favourite Person!

My favourite person is my dog Rocky.
My dog is my favourite because he's funny.
My dog is my favourite because he is cute.
My dog is my favourite because he thinks he's a cat.
My dog is my favourite because he can miaow!

Lilly Grant (10)

My Best Friend

My friend has long blonde hair.
Her eyes are dark, emerald-green.
She has pink lips and curly eyelashes.
She is pretty, tall and wears small pink earrings.
Drawing art is her favourite hobby.
When I fall, she always takes care of me.
Sometimes she wears her hair in many different ways.
She is often very shy but I always get her noticed every time
And she never fails to make me laugh.
I like her and she likes me because she is my best friend.

Kathy McTeague (12)

My Great Nan

Whenever we go to my nan's place,
I always put a smile on her sweet face,
She puts a smile on my face too,
Because that's the kind of magic she can do,
She tells me stories about her from when she was younger,
Then she forgets she's told me them
So she tells me them all over again,
But I just sit and listen,
And watch her eyes glisten,
And I know it's a wonderful memory.

Maisie Dyson (11)

Michael Jackson

You are the star that brightens the night,
You are the rhythm that goes through the people of the world,
You are the beat that goes through everyone's heart and veins,
You are the genius that turned music into fun and dance,
You are the 'King of Pop'!

Joe McGarry (9)

My Mum!

My mum is my favourite person because
She cooks my dinner and tea.
My mum is my favourite person because
She cleans up after me wherever I go.
My mum is my favourite person because
She irons my clothes for me to wear.
My mum is my favourite person because
She gets me ready for school, parties and weddings.
My mum is definitely my favourite person because
She loves me!

Courtney Aston (10)

My Big Sister, Natalie

My big sister is called Natalie
But unfortunately she gave me blisters
She is sometimes the best,
But is often a pest
She is embarrassing most of the time.
I get my revenge by getting slime,
In September I'll be with her in secondary school
I hope she will be the best sister in the whole universe.
She is very clever
And one day she will be at university or college!

Kirsten Perie (11)

My Lop-Eared Friend

This lop-eared friend is always happy,
He's very friendly so he never is snappy,
He sniffs you a lot but never bites,
We have to groom him to protect him from mites,
He always eats his food very, very quick,
I don't know how he does it, it never makes him sick,
When we clean him out there's a lot to be done,
So he jumps around the garden, he finds it great fun,
He follows me, so that makes him very, very clever,
My rabbit named Mercury, is the best pet ever!

Alexandra McMullen (11)

My Furry Friends

My furry friends are gerbils
Their names are Peaches and Ellie
You're in your cage
All day long
Messing about and having fun
You eat and sleep
Stretch and run
And you never complain about being young
And I don't care
Because I know you will always be there.

Carl Knight (10)

My Favourite Person

My favourite person is Mary,
She is very kind,
She buys stuff for me from holiday
She is very pretty.
She has wavy hair
She never falls out with me
We play catch the ball
We go swimming together,
Mary is the best,
We look like twins!

Lucy Lewin (7)

My Super Dad

My dad is number 1
I'm his biggest fan.
I love him so much, he's a great helping hand.

When I'm down he's always there.
Don't we make a brilliant pair?

What would I do without my dad?
He's super, super cool
And also very, very *mad!*
I love my funny, crazy, silly, mad *dad!*

Olivia Leah Donaghue (9)

Toffee (Rabbit)

Toffee is one bouncy boy, big, brown and beautiful
Munching on all the carrots, leaving us none for tea
Tempting us to give him treats with his big eyes
There he goes, off again, into his secret den

When I am sad he knows I am and helps to cheer me up
When I am alone he plays and plays
We have so much fun

I love my rabbit and I will always remember him
As a very playful and cool rabbit.

Sophie Domingo (9)

My Dog Called Saffi

My dog is furry,
My dog is sweet,
My dog is friendly with everyone she meets.

She's a great birdwatcher,
And lover of the sea,
She also likes to play ball with me.

Oh Saffi, oh Saffi,
She's brown with white spots,
She's my best friend and I love her lots.

Megan Vest (10)

My Mum

I love my mum
She is the best
Better than the rest

She could be anything . . .
She could be . . .
A superhero, a fairy
Or a robot, *anything!*

My mum is good at everything . . .
especially good at giving me cuddles.

Eve Allan (9)

My Favourite Person

Picture a flower as colourful
as can be
Picture a warm sunny day
down by the sea
Picture a rainbow, colours
a blast
Picture your favourite thing
 you want to make last . . .

    My mum!

Stacey Graham (11)

My Mum

My mum is the best,
My mum looks after me and my sister,
She keeps us safe and warm,
She works all day and never stops,
I love my mum and she loves me.
That is why she is my favourite person in the world.

Katie Michelle Marder (11)

Usain Bolt

Usain Bolt has the luck of the Jamaicans
He has pure skill,
Skill that kills, that pays the bills.
He is a young man
He has a long time to succeed in his plan,
For new records and show you that he can.
He also has a great imagination
His pose has no agitation,
But it is his speed that draws our appreciation.

Lucy Hickman (9)

Magical Mum

Without my mum I am not a star in the sky
I need to be cheered up when I cry,
When I look at her she makes me smile
When it is bedtime I need someone to tuck me in.
I would die without her by my side
I would make sure my mum is OK
Whatever the cost.
For all the people I love,
I choose my mum.

Daniel Robinson (11)

My Mum, My Favourite

My favourite person is the light of my life.
She spreads her love that shines so bright.
When you need her, she'll be there,
However long she doesn't care.
I can make her mad, I can make her sad,
But most of all I've made her glad
That we'll be together, best friends forever *xxxx*.

Ashleigh Roberts (10)

Michael Jackson Legend

Michael is amazing on stage,
He rocks my world.
I like to think I am just like him.
I like to move and dance like him.
His collection of songs are classic,
It makes my day to hear any of these songs.
Such a shame he died, and a waste of a life
Of someone who had so much to give.
He was such a talented person.

Ellis Scott (8)

Katie Greener – My Favourite Person

Although we're not that close
Katie likes to stand up for me
She is as nice and friendly as a puppy
Plus helpful as well
I wish to think of her in some way
And this poem is to thank her
For her special kindness
School would be a lovely place
If we were all like Katie.

Tanya Brown (9)

My Dad

My best person is my dad
He sells bongos that are not bad
He's always glad
But not when my brother's bad
My dad turns mad
And he wears blue crocs that are very sad
And that's the poem about my dad.

Charlotte Travers (7)

Dad

Dad you help me when I am sad
When I am feeling mad.
You taught me how to subtract and add.
I am not bad
But I am glad
I am proud to be your daughter
I am not embarrassed to say that.
I will not be, forever.
I love you and I will be happy.

Crystal Tueneboah (10)

My Brother Cameron

My brother Cameron,
He is a pest
But I love him so
'Cause he's the best.
He gets up to mischief all the time
But that makes him cheeky
And all mine
What would I do without my little bro?
I will never know.

Annalise Cabrera (12)

My Best Friend Charlie

My best friend ever is Charlie
for he is no longer more
he was a hamster to adore
his fur so white, brown and clean
when he saw me his eyes would gleam.
We used to lie and cuddle a lot of the time
I am so glad that Charlie was mine.

Amy Pritchard (10)

My Favourite Person

She always smells of fresh red roses
Loves to dance and make funny poses.
A permanent smile from ear to ear
She's always there and always near.

'The telly knows everything!' she likes to joke.
Teaching and music are her skills.
She's my favourite person,
My teacher, Mrs Mills!

Harriet Barlow (11)

My Sister

My favourite person is my sister
My sister is sometimes annoying
My sister is sometimes kind
Although she is good or bad, she can't make up a rhythm.

My sister helps me with my homework
When I'm feeling sad and blue
She gives me a hug and says,
I love you!

Matthew Smyth (9)

My Dad

Dads are wonderful things,
They watch films with you,
They even let you sing!

My dad is the best of all,
He is 70 inches tall!
He takes me swimming,
He cooks my tea,
He is the best dad there could ever be!

Jessica Hatton (11)

My Favourite Person

Without her I'm nothing
She's the stars in my bright sky
She looks out for me when I'm hurt
If she left me I would cry.

When it is dark, I am scared
But when she's there I feel safe
She's always by my side
And helps me solve my case.

Liam Robinson (11)

My Mum Brightens

She brightens up the morning,
She brightens up the day.
She brightens up the seaside,
She brightens up the bay.

She brightens up the crack of dawn,
She brightens up the night,
She never ever holds me loose,
She always holds me tight!

Matilda Hancock (10)

Brewster

My greyhound, Brewster, made me smile.
At Wimbledon he could run a mile.
He won lots of prizes, cups and rosettes
But most of all he was our family pet.
When his racing days were over he came home to stay.
We would go to the common where he would play.

Brewster's days are over, he has been laid to rest.
My doggie friend was the very best.

Charlotte Perry (10)

Thank You

T hank you Nanny and Grandad, you are the best
H ow I love you for all that you've done
A nd how I thank you for all the presents you've bought me
N anny, you are the best cook ever
K ind and loving you both are

Y ou are my nanny and grandad
O h I love you
U are the best!

Emily Williams (10)

My Favourite Person

My favourite person is my teacher, Mr Quinton.
He is happy, relaxed and always smiling,
He is never grumpy, moaning or unhappy,
He always listens to you when you have a problem,
And he always helps you solve it!
Mr Quinton is my favourite person,
Most of all he is the best teacher in the world,
That's who my favourite person is!

Courtney Hughes (9)

Fly

My favourite person makes me feel like I could fly.
She makes me happy and this is why.
Lorraine, my dance teacher,
She's my inspiration,
She makes me smile.
I love to dance all day every day,
And she's why.
If only all the children could feel like they could fly!

Chloe Ball (11)

Don't Judge Us!

My name is Emily
And my mum is on her own,
But before you judge us,
I really should say I'm not unhappy or strange,
Well, I hope not,
I'm just like everyone else,
So although my mum is on her own,
Don't judge us!

Emily Forbes (11)

My Mum

I love my mum,
She is the best
She's kind and funny and all the rest.
She makes me laugh,
She makes me smile.
She really would go that extra mile.
She's there for me no matter what,
I love my mum, she beats the rest.

Jerry Durocher-Morris (10)

My Sister

Kathryn, my sister, is special,
She's silly, fun and even clever.
She's got a good sense of music and a good sense of clothes,
But if you pull out a camera she'll definitely pose.
She has two teddy bears called Russell and Sky,
And she plays with them each day that passes by.
So she might be a year younger but we're still best friends forever,
And that's why she's my favourite person ever.

Mirriam Morson (10)

My Worrying, Reassuring Nan!

My nan makes me smile
While I swim across the Nile
My nan gets scared
When I lose my head
My nan's the best
And that's no test
And that's what makes my nan
So worrying and reassuring.

Sukhraj Puwar (12)

It's Me

My favourite person would have to be Dad
He's funky and funny but sometimes goes mad
But my favourite person is often my mum
She's clever and crazy and really good fun
I have to admit it could be my brother
He's weird and wacky, unlike any other
Now I've worked hard on who my best person is
Eureka! I have got it, it's me . . . *Liz!*

Elizabeth Brunt (10)

That's Why They're My Favourite Person

My favourite person is my little brother,
because when I say I'll never do it he'll always says:
'Never say never!'
We'll go through it together.
Always remember I'll love you forever.
I know sometimes we fight,
but we always make it better.
That's why my favourite person is my little brother.

Leah Girvan (9)

My Favourite Person

My name is Darren.
I am in Primary Four.
My favourite person is Lewis
He is cool.
We have lots of fun playing football!
He is my best friend
We have lots of fun at school.
He loves hot dogs and fish and chips.

Darren Slater (8)

All About Callum Walsh

Callum Walsh is the best
And is better than the rest
He will always be my friend
Until the very end
He is a football player
And a very good BMXer
He will always be my best mate
And he will never be late!

Liam Sharland (11)

Michael Jackson, My Hero

Michael Jackson is the best!
He's the coolest,
He's the one who woke the world from its darkest sleep,
Now he's gone, now he's fled,
At least his music still lives on and is rocking the world all over,
His soul is flying around the world checking his kids,
Checking his family and making sure everyone's happy,
I am glad he came into my life.

Jessica Badham (10)

My Friend, Pippa, The Dog

Proudly swaggering around,
Trotting up to me with a big smile on her lovely face.
tail wagging madly.
Walking past her, going to school,
Jumping up at me, making friendly squealing and barking noises
With a splendid, smiling face always pleased to see me.
That is my amazingly, friendly mate Pippa, the lovely dog
With a long, black, slick, twisting body!

Jonathan David Morris (9)

Grandad

My favourite person I never knew
I learnt a lot as I grew
Born in Ukraine far away
Fighting war night and day
A true gentleman as I'm told
For a special grandad I could never hold
My Giddo, I never knew
    I love you.

Kasie Szilak (10)

My Favourite Person

My favourite person would have to be my mum.
She cooks my favourite foods every single day
whilst I go out to play.
When I clean my room, she shouts, 'Hip hip hooray!'

My favourite person would have to be my mum,
she's caring and tells me daily she loves me,
and I say, 'Back at you my favourite mum!'

Kyle Stratford (11)

I Love My Dog

Oh I have a dog called Oliver
He's really cute and cuddly and
I love him very dearly
And I never want to leave him.

When I go out he's at home on his own
And when I go back he's really happy and hyper.
That's why I love my dog.

Natasha Newton (10)

My Mum

My mum is the person I love the most.
She makes me the best toast.
She's got nice clothes and pretty hair
And she cuddles me like a teddy bear.
She takes me out for fun days.
When we went to Longleat we got lost in the maze!

I love my mummy, she's so funny.

Katie Sperring (6)

Frankie

F rankie is the best out of all the rest.
R ound off flick is what she does best.
A ntonia is her sister.
N ice and kind that's what she is.
K indest of all that's what she is.
I think she's great to be a mate.
E mily and Frankie are best friends forever.

Emily Grace Seeds (10)

My Kitten Rocky

My kitten Rocky
Loves to play
Outside in the garden
Every day
When he comes in he miaows to be fed
Then falls asleep
In his comfy cat bed!

Kayleigh Gibson (10)

My Best Friend Ella

My best friend Ella is cool,
We have sleepovers that rule.
Whatever we do we have fun,
We like to play in the sun,
Chatting all day long,
Or even singing a song,
But I say my best friend Ella is cool.

Nicola Finch (10)

The Mum Who Was Good To Me

My mum looks after me like I am her body
She loves me but no matter how cheeky I am
I will never stop loving my kind, loving mother
Until the dawn of death
I love her personality
She touched the heart of me forever and ever
I love my mother!

Sam Young (10)

My Dog Banjo

My dog is woolly and brown and black.
His coat is curly from front to back.
He loves to play with al of his toys.
And he just likes to be one of the boys.
Sometimes he's good, sometimes he's bad,
I love him with all of my heart
Because we are both mad!

Sam Callway (11)

Eddy And Buddy

Eddy and Buddy are my two little puppies,
They sleep nearly all day,
Except when they wake up
For their food and play!
So Eddy and Buddy
Are my two little puppies
And I shall love them forever!

Francesca Johnson (10)

All About My Mum

M y mum is the one who fills my tum when my belly rumbles.
U ndoes my coat, undoes my shoes,
    when I was little, that is what she'd would do.
M um, Mum is the one who loves and cares for you
    and of course my mum is number one.

    Thank you for listening and I hope you had fun.

Shannon Jewell (10)

My Cousin Elise

There once was a girl called Elise,
Who was my mum's niece,
She always liked to sneeze,
When crawling on her knees,
She always had the keys,
That's what made her sneeze.

Holly Gregory (10)

My Favourite Person

My favourite person is my mum
When I was a baby she cleaned my bum
If I was sick she would rub my tummy
When I cried she would give me a dummy
The she would do things I would find funny
And for all this I love my mummy!

Gena-Leigh McNeice (11)

My Favourite Person

My favourite person is kind and gentle
But sometimes she can drive me mental.
And she helps me when I am stuck
And wishes me luck with a test
(Have you guessed who my favourite person is?)
Yes, it is my best friend!

Niamh Berridge-Burley (9)

My Favourite Person

Miss Taplin is the best.
Miss Taplin is beautiful.
She has the longest hair.
When someone is hurt
She takes care of them.
I love her very much!

Freya Lewin (6)

My Favourite Person

My favourite person is my dog.
She may be hairy and smelly
But that doesn't stop me loving her.
I love her and she loves me
And we both live happily in a big family.
I love my dog!

Cailet Latham (11)

My Furry Friend

Mustard the guinea pig sits in his cage looking at me,
I think he is just waiting for his tea.
He has eyes that sparkle in the sun
While he's out in his run.
My very best friend is he
And I know he loves me.

Alexia Dawson (6)

My Cat, Bonnie

B onnie, the three-coloured cat
O range, white and black.
N ags for food, day and night
N ice and friendly, never bites
I mpossible, demanding pest,
E ven so, she's still the best!

Lucy Christian (10)

My Sister

She is a calm sunshine-yellow
She is a lazy autumn afternoon
She is a bobbing boat on the horizon
She is a purring cat hungry for its dinner
She is as tall as a tree waving at me
She is a lovely Christmas morning.

Emily Wallace (11)

Kayleigh

You're a very special friend
You are there to listen
You are there to care
You are a friend who's always there
You are a perfect friend to share my days
You are my friend forever and always.

Rebekah Griffiths (9)

(My Marvellous Mum) My Favourite Person!

My favourite person is my mum,
She shines just like the sun,
She's the rainbow that brightens my day,
In every single way.

Chloe Hawcroft (10)